FACTS AT YOUR FINGERTIPS

AFRICA

BROWN
BEAR
BOOKS

Published by Brown Bear Books Limited

An imprint of
The Brown Reference Group plc
68 Topstone Road
Redding
Connecticut
06896
USA

www.brownreference.com

© 2008 The Brown Reference Group plc

Library of Congress Cataloging-in-Publication Data available upon request.

ISBN-13 978-1-933834-08-5

Author: Derek Hall
Editorial Director: Lindsey Lowe
Project Director: Graham Bateman
Art Director/Design: Steve McCurdy
Editor: Virginia Carter

Printed in Singapore

Picture credits

Cover Images
Front: Sand dunes, Sahara Desert, Morocco (Shutterstock/Sylvaine Thomas)

Back: Fishermen, Zanzibar Island, Tanzania (Shutterstock/Louie Schoeman)

Page 1: Sphinx and pyramid, Egypt (Shutterstock/Izvorinka Jankovic)

Shutterstock:
5 Lynn Amaral; 6 Jonathan Noden-Wilkinson; 8/9 Tonis Valing; 12/13 WH Chow; 26/27 Theunis Jacobus Botha; 38/39 Pichugin Dmitry; 40/41 Kondrachov Vladimir; 42 The Third Man; 46 Styve Reineck; 48/49 Muriel Lasure; 51 Dennis Sabo; 53 Lakis Fourouklas; 56/57 Kim Sarah Bernard; 60 Sapsiwai.

Photos.com:
7, 19, 23, 31, 43, 44, 50, 54/55.

Topfoto.co.uk:
11 ©TopFoto, Silvio Fiore; 16 ©TopFoto; 25 © Alinari/TopFoto. 45 © Topham Picturepoint/TopFoto, Cohen; 58 ©Topham Picturepoint/TopFoto; 59 ©Topham Picturepoint/TopFoto.

eye ubiquitous/Hutchison:
17 Sarah Errington; 20 Tim Beddow; 34/35 Sarah Errington.

The Brown Reference Group has made every effort to trace copyright holders of the pictures used in this book. Anyone having claims to ownership not identified above is invited to contact The Brown Reference Group.

CONTENTS

AFRICA

After Asia, Africa is the second largest of the continents and the second most populous. It comprises not just its continental landmass but also Cape Verde (in the Atlantic) and Madagascar and the Seychelles (in the Indian Ocean). Its largest country is Sudan, its smallest, excluding the Seychelles, is Gambia. The continent is often referred to by regions: North Africa consists of the states abutting the Mediterranean; Central Africa the states of the Sahara (the world's largest desert); West Africa the states of the Atlantic coast, including the Gulf of Guinea; East Africa the states of the Indian Ocean; and Southern Africa the states such as Namibia, South Africa, and Zimbabwe. Today more than 1,000 languages, possibly as many as 2,000, are spoken in Africa.

Early Peoples
Paleoanthropologists consider Africa to be the oldest inhabited territory on Earth, with East Africa being home to apelike humans dating from possibly as early as seven million years ago. More recent fossil remains of *Homo ergaster* date back to about 600,000 to 2,000,000 years B.C. Prehistoric rock paintings have been found in Western Sahara and southern and East Africa. Later finds have included the stone buildings of Great Zimbabwe, bronze sculptures in Benin and Ife, and metalwork from the Ashanti (in today's Ghana). To this list must be added the pyramids and artifacts of ancient Egypt.

Colonial History
Compared to the continent's long prehistory, colonialism in Africa has been a relatively recent phenomenon. There was European trade in gold, ivory, and timber in the 15th and 16th centuries, followed by the notorious slave trade—at its height from the 17th to 19th centuries—but the history of the continent is perhaps best known for its explorers Mungo Park (1771-1806), David Livingstone (1813-73), and Henry Morton Stanley (1841-1904).

Today's Africa
Most states still have the boundaries that were drawn up by Britain, France, Germany, Belgium, Portugal, and other colonizing powers. Many are now republics, operating under a president. Some are democracies, but others have survived successive coups, military dictatorships, violence, and authoritarianism. Matters were further complicated during the Cold War, when both the United States and the Soviet Union sought to impose their influence. The African Union (AU)—a federation of all African states (except Morocco)—was created in 2001 with the aim of transforming the African Economic Community.

Although rich in resources such as oil, gold, and diamonds, Africa's countries are among the world's poorest—often the result of corruption and internal strife. Additionally, parts of sub-Saharan Africa have been overwhelmed by HIV/AIDS. Despite Africa's poverty and violent history, its peoples retain an air of grace and dignity. The peoples of Africa practice a wide range of religious beliefs—mostly Christianity and Islam, but also animism and ancestor worship.

In sport there is a thriving Confederation of African Football, and several countries have reached the knockout stages of the FIFA World Cup. South Africa will host the World Cup in 2010, the first African country to do so. Africa is also known for its long-distance runners—notably those from Ethiopia, Kenya, and Morocco.

Natural Africa
The northern half of Africa is primarily desert, home to nomads and their camels. Primates, including gorillas, live in the tropical rain forest of the western-central region. The remaining central and southern areas comprise grassland and savanna. This is where animals such as lions, cheetahs, leopards, giraffes, zebras, rhinos, and elephants can be found.

Sunset over the African bush. Savanna grassland covers much of southern Africa. The region includes several internationally important game reserves, such as the Kruger National Park.

MOROCCO

One of the few monarchies left in the Arab world, Morocco claims ownership of Western Sahara in the south. The Atlas Mountains form a backbone that runs southwest to northeast, spreading out into the high plateaus toward the Algerian border. In the northwest they slope away to the Atlantic coastal plains—the most fertile region and the site of the principal towns. The main rivers are torrential. Much of Morocco has a temperate Mediterranean climate with hot summers and mild winters, although it is arid and extreme in places.

Most of the population is of Berber descent. The king wields considerable power, being responsible for appointing the prime minister and the supreme court. Agriculture produces one-third of Morocco's exports. Small-scale family farms and government-subsidized cooperatives employ about two-thirds of the workforce, with the main crops being barley, wheat, citrus fruit, and vegetables. Livestock is limited because of poor pastureland. Morocco's main wealth comes from phosphates, of which vast deposits are located in Western Sahara. Chief manufacturing industries include phosphate processing and small-scale industries such as textiles. Fear of terrorism has caused a downturn in tourism, and unemployment is about 23 percent. Graduate unemployment is a major concern, with many qualified Moroccans now seeking work abroad.

The ancient port of Essaouria on the Atlantic coast was founded originally by Phoenician traders in the 7th century B.C. Its architecture reflects Berber, Portuguese, and French cultures.

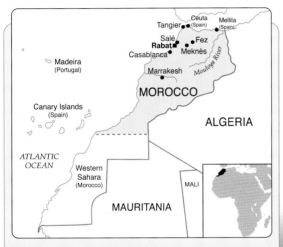

NATIONAL DATA – MOROCCO

Land area	446,300 sq km (172,317 sq mi)			
Climate		Temperatures		Annual
	Altitude m (ft)	January °C(°F)	July °C(°F)	precipitation mm (in)
Rabat	65 (213)	13 (55)	23 (73)	503 (19.8)

Major physical features   highest point: Toubkal 4,165 m (13,665 ft); longest river: Moulouya 595 km (370 mi)

Population   (2006 est.) 33,241,259

Form of government   multiparty constitutional monarchy with one legislative house

Armed forces   army 180,000; navy 7,800; air force 13,000

Largest cities   Casablanca (2,933,684); Rabat (capital – 1,622,860); Fez (946,815)

Official language   Arabic

Ethnic composition   Arab-Berber 99.1%; other 0.7%; Jewish 0.2%

Official religion   Islam

Religious affiliations   Muslim 98.7%; Christian 1.1%; Jewish 0.2%

Currency   1 Moroccan dirham (MAD) = 100 centimes

Gross domestic product   (2006 est.) $147 billion

Gross domestic product per capita   (2006 est.) $4,400

Life expectancy at birth   male 68.62 yr; female 73.37 yr

Major resources   phosphates, iron ore, manganese, lead, zinc, salt, tourism, almonds, cereals, citrus fruits, dates, fish, goats, grapes, olives, poultry, pulses, sheep, timber, vegetables*Not including the Western Sahara

ALGERIA

The second largest country in Africa, Algeria extends from the Mediterranean Sea to the Sahara. The Atlas Mountains bisect the country into two contrasting regions: in the north is an area of coastal plains, rivers, and mountains with a temperate Mediterranean climate—this is the most fertile part of Algeria. To the south of the mountains the land gives way to the arid rocks and sand dunes of the Sahara, making up four-fifths of Algeria's land area. Algeria's path to independence in the 1950s and 1960s was marked by terror campaigns against the ruling French. Violent unrest has often been a feature of political life in more recent times, and even today the minority Muslim Berbers are agitating for autonomy, although this seems unlikely to be granted. Only a small part of the country is sufficiently well watered to be arable, and food imports are needed to make up the shortfall. Drought and locust swarms have posed serious threats to crops in recent years. Mineral resources, especially petroleum and oil, are the mainstay of the economy and attract most of the foreign investment. The government has made it a priority to diversify the economy, and there are plans to modernize fishing along the coast.

Arcaded clay houses at Ghardaia, the chief town of the Mzab oasis in the northern Sahara. The town was founded in the 11th century near the ghar (cave) of the female saint Daia.

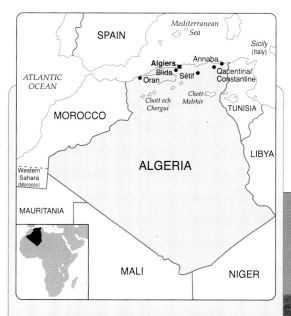

NATIONAL DATA – ALGERIA

Land area 2,381,740 sq km (919,595 sq mi)

Climate	Altitude m (ft)	Temperatures January °C(°F)	Annual July °C(°F)	precipitation mm (in)
Algiers	50 (164)	11 (51)	24 (75)	764 (30)

Major physical features highest point: Mount Tahat 2,918 m (9,573 feet)

Population (2006 est.) 32,930,091

Form of government multiparty republic with one legislative house

Armed forces army 120,000; navy 7,500; air force 10,000

Largest cities Algiers (capital – 1,519,570); Oran (692,516); Qacentina (462,187)

Official language Arabic

Ethnic composition Arab-Berber 99%; European less than 1%

Religious affiliations Sunni Muslim 99%; Christian and Jewish 1%

Currency 1 Algerian dinar (DA) = 100 centimes

Gross domestic product (2006 est.) U.S. $253.4 billion

Gross domestic product per capita (2006 est.) U.S. $7,700

Life expectancy at birth male 71.68 yr; female 74.92 yr

Major resources barley, cattle, citrus fruits, copper, dates, fish, grapes, iron ore, lead, oats, oil and natural gas, olives, phosphates, sheep, timber, uranium, vegetables, wheat, zinc.

TUNISIA

Tunisia is the smallest of the Mediterranean countries of North Africa, sandwiched by its two much larger neighbors, Algeria and Libya. The country has a long history stretching back for 3,000 years, and is among the more liberal of Arab states, taking a nonaligned stance in its foreign relations. However, Islamic fundamentalism, suppressed for many years, is now becoming a more prominent political issue. Throughout much of the later part of its history Tunisia has been heavily influenced by Europe.

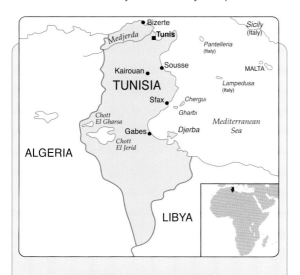

NATIONAL DATA – TUNISIA

Land area	155,360 sq km (59,984 sq mi)			
Climate		Temperatures		Annual precipitation
	Altitude m (ft)	January °C(°F)	July °C(°F)	mm (in)
Tunis	3 (10)	12 (54)	26 (79)	660 (26)

Major physical features highest point: Chambi 1,544 m (5,066 ft); lowest point: Chott El Jerid –23 m (–75 ft)

Population (2006 est.) 10,175,014

Form of government multiparty republic with one legislative house

Armed forces army 27,000; navy 4,800; air force 3,500

Largest cities Tunis (capital – 728,453); Sfax (265,131)

Official language Arabic

Ethnic composition Arab 98%, European 1%; Jewish and other 1%

Religious affiliations Muslim 98%; Christian 1%; Jewish and other 1%

Currency 1 Tunisian dinar (D) = 1,000 millimes

Gross domestic product (2006 est.) U.S. $87.88 billion

Gross domestic product per capita (2006 est.) U.S. $8,600

Life expectancy at birth male 73.4 yr; female 76.96 yr

Major resources petroleum, natural gas, phosphates, iron ore, lead, zinc, tourism, fruits, olive oil, barley, cork, dates, fish, grapes, livestock, olives, salt, timber, tomatoes, wheat

Geography

Tunisia is bisected by the eastern end of the Atlas Mountains. They form a continuous plateau (the Dorsale) extending northeast from the Algerian border to the plains bordering the Gulf of Tunis. To the south are high steppes and hills, beyond which the terrain becomes flat and dry. The few rivers are seasonal, and the country is dotted with salt flats that are dry in summer but that become treacherous bogs in winter. The southeast of Tunisia merges quickly with the Sahara. In the north the Medjerda River flows down the Dorsale through a fertile valley formed from ancient lake basins and enters the Gulf of Tunis via a broad, coastal plain. Tunisia enjoys a hot, Mediterranean climate; summers are hot and winters mild. Most rainfall occurs in winter. Hardy esparto grass clads the steppes south of the Atlas range, but this gives way to scrub

The monumental Roman amphitheater at El Jem is the third largest in the world and the best-preserved Roman relic in Africa.

Economy

Apart from oil-rich Libya, Tunisia has a higher standard of living than the rest of North Africa, with 60 percent of the population being recognized as "middle class." Although agriculture is still the largest single employer, the industry has declined in recent years. and now provides only around 14 percent of GNP. The north has been a grain-growing region since Roman times and produces wheat and barley as well as olives, citrus fruit, grapes, sugar beet, and vegetables. Forestry produces valuable quantities of cork as well as eucalyptus and other oils. Livestock rearing is limited by the poor pastureland and consists chiefly of goats and sheep, with camels as work animals.

Minerals, especially phosphates and petroleum, are an important source of national wealth. Both are exported, together with natural gas, but fluctuating world prices have depressed this sector of the economy. Industrial production is based on these commodities as well as on olive oil production and other manufacturing industries such as textiles. Some heavy manufacturing has been set up with foreign investment. The country has extensive rail and road networks, although these are in need of modernization. Tunisia has long relied on tourism as its main foreign currency earner. Its equable climate, sunny beaches, and historic sights attract visitors from many parts of the world. However, the recent conflicts in the Middle East and the rise of Islamic terrorism have reduced this valuable industry.

TUNISIA'S VARIED RULERS

The capital city Tunis lies on the site of Carthage, the ancient trading city of the Phoenicians that dominated the western Mediterranean until its destruction by the Romans in the 2nd century B.C. From the 7th century A.D. the surrounding area was part of the Muslim Arab empire, and in the 16th century it was incorporated into the Ottoman Empire as a semi-independent principality. Economic stagnation in the 19th century caused the country to become hugely indebted, and France used this as an excuse to seize control of the country in 1881. Independence was gained in 1957.

and then desert. In the north large forested areas, mainly of Aleppo pine, are found on the slopes of the Dorsale, giving way to broadleaved trees in the valleys. Lynx and boars inhabit the forests, while farther south jackals, hyenas, and birds such as eagles flourish.

Society

The Tunisian people are basically Arab, mixed with Berber and a wide range of other Mediterranean and African peoples. Virtually the whole population of the country is Muslim; the once large Jewish community has almost completely emigrated. Although a progressive and open society compared with many other Arab states, Tunisia is *de facto* a one-party dictatorship.

Libya is a rich country with a high standard of living. Both its wealth and its energy are derived from vigorous exploitation of its oil reserves under government control. Its leader, Colonel Muammar Qaddafi (b. 1942), led the overthrow of the monarchy in 1969 in a military coup and retains control as "Revolutionary Leader" with the help of the armed forces and close advisers.

NATIONAL DATA – LIBYAN ARAB JAMAHIRIYA

Land area   1,759,540 sq km (679,362 sq mi)

Climate	Altitude m (ft)	Temperatures January °C(°F)	July °C(°F)	Annual precipitation mm (in)
Tripoli	50 (164)	14 (57)	26 (80)	272 (10.7)

Major physical features   highest point: Bette 2,286 m (7,500 ft)

Population   (2006 est.) 5,900,754

Form of government   Jamahiriya a "state of the masses"–in practice a one-party state and military dictatorship

Armed forces   army 54,000; navy 8,000; air force 23,000

Largest cities   Tripoli (capital – 1,178,007); Benghazi (950,000); Misurata (300,000); al-Aziziyah (287,407)

Official language   Arabic

Ethnic composition   Berber and Arab 97%; Greeks, Maltese, Italians, Egyptians, Pakistanis, Turks, Indians, Tunisians 3.0%

Official religion   Islam

Religious affiliations   Sunni Muslim 97.0%; others 3.0%

Currency   1 Libyan dinar (LD) = 1,000 dirhams

Gross domestic product   (2006 est.) U.S. $74.97 billion

Gross domestic product per capita   (2006 est.) U.S. $12,700

Life expectancy at birth   male 74.46 yr; female 79.02 yr

Major resources   petroleum, natural gas, cement, iron ore, gypsum, barley, citrus fruits, dates, figs, groundnuts, livestock, olives, sorghum, tobacco, wheat

Geography

Over nine-tenths of Libya's land area is desert or semidesert, and more than three-quarters of the population lives along the narrow coastal strip where the Sahara gives way to cultivation. Tripolitana, a large area in the northwest, extends eastward from the border with Tunisia. Here the mountains of Jabal Nafusah lie between the Sahara and the dunes, saltmarshes, and steppe of the Gefara Plain. The Gefara Plain is the most fertile spot and the site of Tripoli. Southward, in the area called Fezzan, the Sahara rises to the edge of the North African plateau, bordering Algeria. Libya's highest mountain, Bette, is part of the Tibesti Mountains that span the border with Chad. Libya's desert climate has intensely hot days and cold nights, but this is moderated along the Mediterranean coast. Rainfall is sporadic, and droughts can occur even on the coast. Vegetation is mainly sparse steppe grassland, scrub, and date palms near oases. Wildlife is predominantly desert-dwelling species like jackals, jerboas, and fennec foxes.

Society

Throughout its history parts of Libya have been under the control of the empires of Carthage, Greece, Rome, the Byzantines, and the Turks, as well as the British and the French. Today most Libyans are Arabic-speaking Sunni Muslims of mixed Arab and Berber descent. There are also small groups of nomadic Tuaregs. Migration from sub-Saharan Africa has considerably swelled the numbers of foreign workers in several major cities.

Economy

Agriculture employs about one-fifth of the workforce, but Libya is not self-sufficient in food and imports about 75 percent of its needs. Arable land is limited and intensively farmed, but irrigation is difficult. Cereals such as barley form the major crop; sorghum is grown in Fezzan, and wheat, tobacco, and olives are raised in the north. In the oases dates and figs are cultivated, and grapes are grown in the north. Sheep, goats, and cattle are reared in the north as well.

The Libyan economy depends mainly on its oil reserves for its wealth. Petroleum and natural gas account for about one-third of the country's GDP and

An oasis in Fezzan, in the southwest of Libya. Oases are fertile, water-fed areas in otherwise arid stretches of desert.

practically all export earnings. The assets of most foreign oil companies were nationalized in 1973, and the state retains a controlling interest in new ventures. Coupled with a small population, the oil revenues give Libya one of the highest per capita GDPs in Africa, although little of this income benefits the average citizen. Cement production and iron ore extraction are likewise state controlled. All of Libya's energy comes from domestic oil, although Niger has supplied uranium for a proposed nuclear power station. Manufacturing is small-scale, and mainly centered on textiles, footwear, and carpets. In recent years economic reforms and privatization initiatives have been instigated as part of Libya's rehabilitation into the international community. The Great Man-made River Project, the world's biggest water development scheme, is being built to bring water from large aquifers under the Sahara to coastal cities.

INTERNATIONAL REHABILITATION

In the past Libya has openly supported terrorist organizations—notably extremist Palestinian groups—in the name of Arab nationalism and the destruction of capitalism. Suspected Libyan involvement in major terrorist incidents led to an American air raid on Tripoli in 1986, and international sanctions against Libya were imposed in 1992. Libya began to rebuild relationships with Europe during the 1990s and make reparations for some of its involvement in terrorism. In 2003 sanctions were lifted after Libya announced the end of its program for the development of weapons of mass destruction.

EGYPT

Egypt lies in the northeastern corner of Africa, with its northern border on the Mediterranean and its eastern border washed by the waters of the Red Sea. The country boasts one of the world's oldest continuous civilizations, with an historical legacy of monumental importance in the development of mankind. Today this Arab republic retains its distinctive society and culture.

NATIONAL DATA – COUNTRY

Land area	995,450 sq km (384,343 sq mi)			

Climate	Altitude m (ft)	Temperatures January °C(°F)	July °C(°F)	Annual precipitation mm (in)
Cairo	75 (246)	14 (54)	28 (83)	25 (1)

Major physical features highest point: Mount Catherine 2,637 m (8,652 ft); longest river: Nile (part) 6,690 km (4,160 mi)

Population (2006 est.) 78,887,007

Form of government single-party republic with one legislative house

Armed forces army 340,000; navy 18,500; air force 30,000

Largest cities Cairo (capital – 15,707,992); Alexandria (4,320,129); Giza (1,560,024)

Official language Arabic

Ethnic composition Egyptian 98%; Berber, Nubian, Bedouin, and Beja 1%; Greek, Armenian, other European (mainly Italian and French) 1%

Official religion Islam

Religious affiliations Muslim (mostly Sunni) 90%; Coptic 9%; other Christian 1%

Currency 1 Egyptian pound (EGP or LE) = 100 piastres = 1,000 millièmes

Gross domestic product (2006 est.) U.S. $328.1 billion

Gross domestic product per capita (2006 est.) U.S. $4,200

Life expectancy at birth male 68.77 yr; female 73.93 yr

Major resources petroleum, natural gas, iron ore, phosphates, manganese, gypsum, limestone, talc, asbestos, lead, zinc, tourism, barley, beans, buffaloes, cattle, clover, cotton, dates. goats, gypsum, lentils, maize/corn, millet, rice, sea salt, sugarcane, sheep

Geography

Approximately two-thirds of Egypt consists of a huge arid plateau known as the Western Desert. To the southwest, outcrops of land rise to some 2,000 m (7,000 ft). To the east lies the Nile Valley—a fertile strip of land only 16 km (10 mi) across at its widest. The majority of the population live here and still rely on the Nile today—as they did in the past—as a vital source of water and a means of transport. The amount of fertile soils that wash down on the floods has been reduced since the completion of the Aswan High Dam in 1971, however, changing the Nile's role in the agriculture and economy of the country. The great river flows northward to form a vast delta extending from Cairo to the coastal towns of Alexandria in the west and Port Said in the east. The northernmost extension of the Red Sea is the Gulf of Suez, linked to Port Said and the Mediterranean by the Suez Canal. An extension of the Ethiopian Highlands, the Red Sea

Mountains, run along the southeast coast. The hot desert climate is moderated only by the Mediterranean in the north. Water plants and birds such as ibises and egrets abound along the Nile, and in the desert hyenas, jackals, scorpions, and other desert species are found.

Society

A series of dynasties ruled Egypt for three millennia, from about 3200 B.C. Then Egypt was ruled by Greeks, Romans, Byzantines, Arabs, and Ottoman Turks, and the country declined culturally and economically. Britain took control of Egypt in 1882 to protect its investments in the country, but nominal allegiance to the Ottoman Empire continued until 1914. By 1922 Egypt had become partially independent of Britain, and fully so after World War II. Gamal Nasser (1918–70) seized power in 1954 and nationalized the Suez Canal, resulting in an abortive invasion by Britain, France, and Israel. Friendlier relations with the West were established under Anwar Sadat (1918–81), while

The second Great Pyramid at Giza, near Cairo, marks the tomb of the pharaoh Khafre. It dates from the 26th century B.C. and contains 2 million blocks of limestone. In front of it stands the Sphinx, whose weathered face is believed to depict Khafre.

EGYPT'S TWO GREAT WATERWAYS

The Nile River is Egypt's lifeblood, used for irrigation and transportation. For thousands of years its floods have brought fertile silt to a valley 8–16 km (5–10 mi) wide that cuts through the surrounding desert. Almost 90 percent of the population lives in this narrow strip of land. In the south the Aswan High Dam, built across the Nile, has created the vast Lake Nasser. The Suez Canal, built in northeastern Egypt between 1859 and 1969, linked the Mediterranean Sea and the Indian Ocean and gave Egypt new strategic importance, although many supertankers are now too big to use it.

---

dependence on the Soviet Union was ended. Egypt is the world's most populous Arab country, and Cairo, the capital, is the most highly populated city in Africa.

Economy

Egypt's economy depends mainly on agriculture, petroleum, and services, with petroleum and its products making up half of exports. The main crops are cotton (Egypt produces one-third of the world's cotton) and sugarcane, but the country also grows millet, beans, and dates. Fishing thrives, but has declined in the Mediterranean, probably as a result of changing waterflow patterns caused by the Aswan High Dam. Industries such as petroleum and natural gas extraction produce about one-third of GDP and employ some 17 percent of the workforce. Despite terrorist attacks on tourist sites, tourism continues to be a major source of revenue for the country. Other important sectors include the media and various forms of manufacturing.

Egypt's rapidly growing population and migration to the cities, coupled with limited arable land (less than 3 percent is farmed) and the need for food subsidies, continue to drain resources. Yet increased tourism and huge overseas investments have helped develop the infrastructure, and economic conditions are improving after many years when little progress was made. The state employs about one-third of the workforce, and some 5 million Egyptian nationals work abroad, especially in Saudi Arabia, the Gulf states, and Europe.

WESTERN SAHARA

Western Sahara is a mostly flat, desert land with large, rocky areas rising to low mountains in the south and northeast. Its main natural resources are phosphates and iron ore, although the coast is rich in fish. Most agriculture is in the form of pastoral nomadism, with fruits and vegetables grown in the few oases, and camels, goats, and sheep grazed on suitable pastureland. Phosphate mining is the main industry.

The territory has long been the subject of disputed ownership; Morocco lays claim to it and controls economic activity, having annexed the land between 1976 and 1979. However, a guerrilla war waged by the Polisario Front contested Morocco's sovereignty. It ended in a 1991 UN-brokered ceasefire, although a referendum on the region's final status has still to be held.

NATIONAL DATA – WESTERN SAHARA

Land area	266,000 sq km (102,703 sq mi)
Climate	Arid
Population	(2006 est.) 273,008
Form of government	Status and sovereignty unresolved; territory contested by Morocco and Polisario Front (Popular Front for the Liberation of the Saguia el Hamra and Rio de Oro)
Largest city	al-Ayun (188,084)
Official languages	Arabic, Spanish
Ethnic composition	Predominantly Arab Berber; but also Afro-Arab, South Asians, Europeans
Religious affiliations	100% Muslim
Currency	1 Moroccan Dirham (MAD) = 100 centimes
Major resources	phosphates, iron ore, dried fish

MAURITANIA

Behind Mauritania's coastal plains there are higher plateaus with occasional peaks and scarps. However, most of the land consists of the Sahara. The extreme south forms part of the notorious drought-ridden Sahel region. Since independence the country has experienced violence from Polisario guerrillas based in Western Sahara, coups, and tensions between its black and Arab-Berber populations. Half the people depend on farming for a living. Mauritania's extensive iron ore deposits account for nearly 40 percent of total exports.

NATIONAL DATA – MAURITANIA

Land area	1,030,400 sq km (397, 840 sq mi)

Climate	Altitude m (ft)	Temperatures January °C(°F)	July °C(°F)	Annual precipitation mm (in)
Nouakchott	1 (3)	22 (72)	28 (83)	159 (6.2)

Major physical features	highest point: Kediat Idjil 915 m (3,002 ft)
Population	(2006 est.) 3,177,388
Form of government	multiparty republic with two legislative houses
Armed forces	army 15,000; navy 620; air force 250
Capital city	Nouakchott (881,000)
Official language	Arabic
Ethnic composition	Mixed Maur/black 40%; Moor 30%; Black 30%
Official religion	Islam
Religious affiliations	100% Sunni Muslim
Currency	1 ouguiya (MRO) = 5 Khoums
Gross domestic product	(2006 est.) U.S. $8.397 billion
Gross domestic product per capita	(2006 est.) U.S. $2,600
Life expectancy at birth	male 50.88 yr; female 55.42 yr
Major resources	iron ore, gypsum, copper, phosphate, diamonds, gold, oil, fish, dates, livestock, millet, rice, salt, sorghum, wheat

MALI

Mali lies in the Sahel region of North Africa. About 70 percent of the land is desert or semidesert. Droughts have ravaged the region in recent years, and only the southern part of the country, crossed by the Niger River and its tributaries, supports significant animal and plant life. Mali's arable land is also in the south, but only consists of one-fiftieth of the total land area. Industrial activity is centered on processing agricultural produce; its minerals are underexploited. At the turn of the 21st century Mali was one of the world's 10 poorest countries, and it relies heavily on foreign aid.

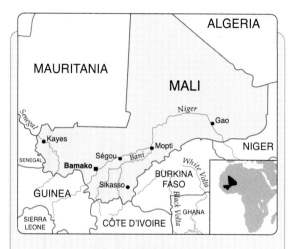

NATIONAL DATA – MALI

Land area 1,220,000 sq km (471,045 sq mi)

Climate	Altitude m (ft)	Temperatures January °C(°F)	July °C(°F)	Annual precipitation mm (in)
Bamako	331 (1,086)	25 (77)	27 (81)	991 (39)

Major physical features highest point: Hombori Tondo 1,155 m (3,789 ft); longest river: Niger (part) 4,200 km (2,600 mi)

Population (2006 est.) 11,716,829

Form of government multiparty republic with one legislative house

Armed forces army 7,350; paramilitary 4,800; inactive militia 3,000

Largest cities Bamako (capital – 1, 690,471); Sikasso (154,823); Mopti (112,248); Koutiala (106,857); Kayes (103,797)

Official language French

Ethnic composition Mande 50% (Bambara, Malinke, Soninke); Peul 17%; Voltaic 12%; Songhai 6%; Tuareg and Moor 10%; other 5%

Religious affiliations Muslim 90%; indigenous beliefs 9%; Christian 1%

Currency 1 Communauté Financière Africaine franc (XOF) = 100 centimes

Gross domestic product (2006 est.) U.S. $14.59 billion

Gross domestic product per capita (2006 est.) U.S. $1,200

Life expectancy at birth male 47.05 yr; female 51.01 yr

Major resources gold, phosphates, kaolin, salt, limestone, uranium, gypsum, granite, hydropower, bauxite, iron ore, manganese, tin, copper

NIGER

Part of the drought-ridden Sahel region, Niger is one of the poorest countries in the world, with a poor infrastructure and 63 percent of the population below the poverty line. Two-thirds of the country consists of the Sahara, with only the southwest, around the Niger River valley, having any useful arable land. The majority of the population lives in the south. With few surfaced roads, camel trains are still a vital way of transporting goods across the country. About 90 percent of the people are employed in subsistence agriculture.

NATIONAL DATA – NIGER

Land area 1,266,700 sq km (489,076 sq mi)

Climate	Altitude m (ft)	Temperatures January °C(°F)	July °C(°F)	Annual precipitation mm (in)
Niamey	222 (728)	26 (80)	29 (84)	541 (21.2)

Major physical features highest point: Mont Gréboun 1,944 m (6,378 ft); longest river: Niger (part) 4,200 km (2,600 mi)

Population (2006 est.) 12,525,094

Form of government multiparty republic with one legislative house

Armed forces army 5,200; air force 100

Largest cities Niamey (capital – 707,951); Zinder (170,575); Maradi (148,017); Agadez (78,289); Arlit (69,435)

Official language French

Ethnic composition Hausa 56%; Djerma 22%; Fula 8.5%; Tuareg 8%; Beri Beri (Kanouri) 4.3%; Arab, Toubou, and Gourmantche 1.2%

Religious affiliations Muslim 80%; traditional beliefs and Christian 20%

Currency 1 Communauté Financière Africaine franc (XOF) = 100 centimes

Gross domestic product (2006 est.) U.S. $12.23 billion

Gross domestic product per capita (2006 est.) U.S. $1,000

Life expectancy at birth male 43.8 yr; female 43.73 yr

Major resources uranium, coal, iron ore, tin, phosphates, gold, molybdenum, gypsum, salt, petroleum, cotton, groundnuts, livestock, millet, rice, sorghum

CHAD

Straddling the drought-stricken Sahel region of North Africa, landlocked Chad is a country of wide, dry central plains rising from the Chad Basin in the southeast to the volcanic Tibesti Mountains in the north and the Ennedi plateau and Ouaddai Mountains in the east. The climate is tropical and hot. Summer rains support fertile savanna and broadleaved trees in the south, which has relatively abundant and diverse wildlife. Rainfall diminishes farther north, however, and the northern third of the country is arid scrub or desert. The country is a melting pot of peoples, with more than 100 different languages spoken. Since 2003 fighting between the Janjawid armed militia, Sudanese military, and rebel groups in western Sudan have driven about 200,000 refugees from Darfur into eastern Chad, which has played an important role as a mediator in the Sudanese civil conflict.

Agriculture employs about four-fifths of the workforce and provides about half the GDP. The country is self-sufficient in food when there are no droughts. Livestock is the most important export. Petroleum is the major resource, and a pipeline built with World Bank funding has enabled Chad to export this commodity.

Papyrus boats on Lake Chad. Lake Chad is the only large body of standing water in the country. Shallow and marshy, the lake once covered a larger area but is shrinking as the Sahara advances into the region.

NATIONAL DATA – CHAD

Land area	1,259,200 sq km (486,180 sq mi)			

Climate	Altitude m (ft)	Temperatures January °C(°F)	July °C(°F)	Annual precipitation mm (in)
N'Djamena	295 (968)	21 (70)	26 (79)	510 (20)

Major physical features highest point: Emi Koussi 3,415 m (11,204 ft); longest river: Chari 949 km (590 mi)

Population (2006 est.) 9,944,201

Form of government multiparty republic with one legislative house

Armed forces army 25,000; air force 350

Capital city N'Djamena (753,791)

Official languages Arabic, French

Ethnic composition Sara/Bagirmi/Kreish 30.5%; Sudanic Arab 26.1%; Teda 7.3%; Mbum 6.5%; Masalit/Maba/Mimi 6.3%; Mubi 4.2%; Kanuri 2.3%; Hausa 2.3%; Masa 2.3%; Kotoko 2.1%; others 10.1%

Religious affiliations Muslim 51%; Christian 35%; animist 7%; other 7%

Currency 1 Communauté Financière Africaine franc (XAF) = 100 centimes

Gross domestic product (2006 est.) U.S. $15.26 billion

Gross domestic product per capita (2006 est.) U.S. $1,500

Life expectancy at birth male 45.88 yr; female 49.21 yr

Major resources petroleum, uranium, natron, kaolin, fish (Lake Chad), gold, limestone, sand and gravel, salt, cassava, cattle, cotton, dates, gum Arabic, millet, groundnuts, rice, sorghum, sweet potatoes, yams

SUDAN

Africa's largest state, Sudan extends from just south of the Tropic of Cancer to just north of the equator. For thousands of years it formed a trade bridge between southern Africa and the Mediterranean, yet today it is one of the least developed countries in the world. In common with other countries in the region, social welfare is only limited, and there are few

A refugee camp in northeast Sudan. Fighting in the Darfur region between rebel groups and government forces backed by Janjawid guerrillas has led to massive displacement of innocent civilians.

NATIONAL DATA – SUDAN

Land area	2,376,000 sq km (917,379 sq mi)			
Climate		Temperatures		Annual
	Altitude m (ft)	January °C(°F)	July °C(°F)	precipitation mm (in)
Khartoum	380 (1,247)	23 (74)	32 (90)	162 (6.3)

Major physical features highest point: Kinyeti 3,187 m (10,456 ft); longest river: Nile (part) 6,690 km (4,160 mi)

Population (2006 est.) 41,236,378

Form of government multiparty republic with one legislative house

Armed forces army 100,000; navy 1,800; air force 3,000

Largest cities Omdurman (3,127,802); Khartoum (capital – 2,207,794); Khartoum Bahri (1,725,570)

Official language Arabic

Ethnic composition Black 52%; Arab 39%; Beja 6%; other 3%

Religious affiliations Sunni Muslim 70% (in north); traditional beliefs 25%; Christian 5%

Currency 1 Sudanese dinar (SDD) = 10 Sudanese pounds, which are each further subdivided into 100 piastres

Gross domestic product (2006 est.) U.S. $96.01 billion

Gross domestic product per capita (2006 est.) U.S. $2,300

Life expectancy at birth male 57.69 yr; female 60.21 yr

Major resources petroleum, iron ore, copper, chromium ore, zinc, tungsten, mica, silver, gold, hydropower, beans, cotton, natural gas, dates, groundnuts, gum Arabic, livestock, sesame seeds, sorghum, wheat

healthcare facilities. Sudan's landscape ranges from harsh desert in the north, interrupted only by a thin line of cultivation along the Nile River, to mountains and dense rain forests in the south, supporting wildlife such as chimps, hippos, elephants, lions, and leopards. The central southern area is savanna and shrubland, with papyrus swamps. The north has a tropical climate and almost no rainfall, with the heat only moderated along the Red Sea coast. The far south has a hot, equatorial climate with high rainfall.

Wars and famine have ravaged Sudan for decades; over 2 million people have died as a result of these afflictions since 1983. The ongoing genocide in Darfur in western Sudan between government forces and Arab militias known as Janjawid on the one hand, and rebel groups on the other, has led to many thousands of deaths and displacements and calls for effective UN intervention to uphold a ceasefire. The internal conflicts have seriously damaged Sudan's ability to build a strong economy. Agriculture employs most of the workforce, with cotton, millet, and groundnuts among the crops grown. Oil production began in 1998. Textiles, shoes, soap, and beverages are also manufactured.

The smallest country in northern Africa, Djibouti has a strategic location close to the world's busiest shipping lanes and near to Arabian oil fields. Djibouti is one of the world's hottest countries. The heartland and south are dominated by volcanic plateaus, while in the north there are mountains. A few mountainous areas are wooded, but most places are scrub or desert. Much of the population lives in the capital; the rest are nomadic herders. The economy is centered on service activities based on Djibouti's strategic location as a transit port for the region and as an international transshipment and refueling hub, but it still depends on foreign aid.

Eritrea's landscape is dominated by an extension of the Ethiopian Highlands, descending in the east to a coastal plain, in the southwest to rolling plains, and in the northwest to hills. Eritrea gained UN recognition as an independent country in 1993 after a 30-year war of independence with Ethiopia that left the new nation famine-struck and with no real infrastructure. Peace was brokered by the UN after hostilities later resumed between Eritrea and Ethiopia. A small and desperately poor country, Eritrea relies largely on subsistence farming, although there is a tiny but outdated industrial sector. Money sent home by Eritreans working abroad makes a significant contribution to GDP.

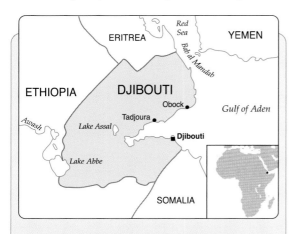

NATIONAL DATA – DJIBOUTI

Land area	22,980 sq km (8,873 sq mi)			
Climate		Temperatures		Annual
	Altitude m (ft)	January °C(°F)	July °C(°F)	precipitation mm (in)
Djibouti	8 (26)	25 (74)	36 (97)	164 (6.4)

Major physical features highest point: Musa Ali Terara 2,063 m (6,768 ft); lowest point: Lake Assal –150 m (–492 ft)

Population (2006 est.) 486,530

Form of government multiparty republic with one legislative house

Armed forces army 8,000; navy 200; air force 250

Capital city Djibouti (317,000)

Official languages Arabic, French

Ethnic composition Somali 60%; Afar 35%; French, Arab, Ethiopian, and Italian 5%

Religious affiliations Muslim 94%; Christian 6%

Currency Djiboutian franc (DJF) = 100 centimes

Gross domestic product (2002 est.) U.S. $619 million

Gross domestic product per capita (2005 est.) U.S. $1,000

Life expectancy at birth male 41.86 yr; female 44.52 yr

Major resources geothermal power, gold, clay, granite, limestone, marble, salt, diatomite, gypsum, pumice, petroleum, cattle, dates, fish, fruit and vegetables, goats, sheep

NATIONAL DATA – ERITREA

Land area	121,320 sq km (46,842 sq mi)			
Climate		Temperatures		Annual
	Altitude m (ft)	January °C(°F)	July °C(°F)	precipitation mm (in)
Asmara	2,335 (7,661)	14 (57)	17 (62)	533 (21)

Major physical features highest point: Monte Soira 2,989 m (9,807 ft)

Population (2006 est.) 4,786,994

Form of government transitional

Armed forces army 200,000; navy 1,400; air force 350

Capital city Asmara (500,600)

Official languages Tigrinya and Arabic

Ethnic composition ethnic Tigrinya 50%; Tigre and Kunama 40%; Afar 4%; Saho (Red Sea coast dwellers) 3%; other 3%

Religious affiliations Muslim; Coptic Christian; Roman Catholic; Protestant

Currency 1 nafka (ERN) = 100 cents

Gross domestic product (2005 est.) U.S. $4.471 billion

Gross domestic product per capita (2005 est.) U.S. $1,000

Life expectancy at birth male 57.44 yr; female 60.66 yr

Major resources gold, potash, zinc, copper, salt, unexploited oil and natural gas, fish, barley, beans and peas, cattle, coffee, cotton, maize/corn, millet, platinum, sorghum, sugarcane, timber, wheat

ETHIOPIA

In the 16th and 17th centuries the fortress-city of Fasil Ghebbi at Gondor in the foothills of the Simien Mountains was the home of the Ethiopian emperor Fasilides and his successors.

Ethiopia lies on a plateau bisected by the Great Rift Valley. To the west the land rises up to 3,700 m (12,000 ft). From Lake Tana in the northwest the Blue Nile gorge cuts a winding course. In the north the Simen Mountains rise to Ras Dashan, the highest peak, then drop away to the narrow Red Sea coastal plain. There are volcanoes in the north and south. The vegetation varies from tropical rain forests to lowlying savanna. Rainfall is highest in the south and west, but it is the droughts in the north that have made the country synonymous with famine. Following neighboring Eritrea's independence from Ethiopia in 1993, further outbreaks of fighting between the two countries were finally halted by a peace treaty in 2000. However, the boundary agreements vital to this peace treaty are currently disputed by Ethiopia.

Ethiopia is one of the poorest and one of the most indebted nations in the world, with a declining economy. Some 4 million people rely on food assistance annually. Agriculture employs about four-fifths of the workforce, but output has been severely reduced by wars and drought. The main export crop is coffee, but low prices have depressed this sector.

NATIONAL DATA – ETHIOPIA

Land area 1,119,683 sq km (432,312 sq mi)

Climate	Altitude m (ft)	Temperatures January °C(°F)	July °C(°F)	Annual precipitation mm (in)
Addis Ababa	2,360 (7,741)	20 (67)	20 (67)	1,020 (40.1)

Major physical features highest point: Ras Dashan 4,620 m (15,158 ft)

Population (2006 est.) 74,777,981

Form of government one-party federal republic with one legislative house

Armed forces army 180,000; air force 2,500

Largest cities Addis Ababa (capital – 2,973,000); Dire Dawa (281,800); Nazret (228,600); Bahir Dar (167,300)

Official language Amharic

Ethnic composition Oromo 40%; Amhara and Tigre 32%; Sidamo 9%; Shankella 6%; Somali 6%; Afar 4%; Gurage 2%; other 1%

Religious affiliations Muslim 45%-50%; Ethiopian Orthodox 35%-40%; animist 12%; other 3%-8%

Currency 1 Ethiopian birr (ETB) = 100 cents

Gross domestic product (2006 est.) U.S. $71.63 billion

Gross domestic product per capita (2006 est.) U.S. $1,000

Life expectancy at birth male 47.86 yr; female 50.24 yr

Major resources small reserves of gold, platinum, copper, natural gas, hydropower, barley, beans and peas, cattle, coffee, cotton, maize/corn, millet, potash, salt, sorghum, sugarcane, timber, wheat

SOMALIA

Somalia lies along the Horn of Africa, a huge promontory on the northeastern coast. The Guban, the narrow coastal plain, is hot, barren scrubland. The Ogo Highlands lie to the north, and to the south lies the Haud Plateau, beyond which the land slopes toward the Indian Ocean. The two main rivers, the Juba and the Shebelle, provide the south with a vital water resource in what is an almost constantly hot and inhospitable arid climate. Small forests and grassland grow on the northern slopes and in parts of the south, but elsewhere Somalia is semidesert or dry savanna.

Somalia was probably the "land of Punt" referred to in the Bible. More than two-thirds of the population are descendants of Arab and Persian traders. The Somali Republic became independent in 1960, but the president was assassinated in a coup and replaced by Siyad Barre (1919–95), who was ousted in 1991. Factional fighting and anarchy have followed, despite the formation of a transitional federal government. Somalia has also been linked with global terrorism.

Despite political turmoil, economic activity continues—largely because most of it is in the form of local, pastoral, and nomadic agriculture. Arable farming is confined on the whole to the region between the two main rivers, covering less than one-fiftieth of the overall area. Crops include maize/corn, groundnuts, sugarcane, and bananas. Concerns about Rift Valley Fever caused Saudi Arabia to ban imports of Somali livestock, a severe blow to its economy. Somalia's small industrial sector, based mainly on the processing of agricultural products and petroleum, remains seriously disrupted.

About half of Somalia's land supports the nomadic herding of camels, cattle, and goats.

NATIONAL DATA – SOMALIA

Land area	627,337 sq km (242,216 sq mi)			

Climate	Altitude m (ft)	Temperatures January °C(°F)	July °C(°F)	Annual precipitation mm (in)
Mogadishu	17 (56)	27 (81)	26 (79)	427 (17)

Major physical features highest point: Surud Ad 2,406 m (7,894 ft); longest river: Shebelle (part) 2,010 km (1,250 mi)

Population (2006 est.) 8,863,338

Form of government transitional

Armed forces no national armed forces

Largest cities Mogadishu (capital – 2,855,805); Hargeysa (522,508); Marka (350,859); Berbera (263,095)

Official language Somali

Ethnic composition Somali 85%; Bantu and other non-Somali 15% (including Arabs 30,000)

Religious affiliations 100% Sunni Muslim

Currency 1 Somali shilling (SOS) = 100 cents

Gross domestic product (2006 est.) U.S. $5.023 billion

Gross domestic product per capita (2006 est.) U.S. $600

Life expectancy at birth male 46.71 yr; female 50.28 yr

Major resources uranium and largely unexploited reserves of iron ore, tin, gypsum, bauxite, copper, salt, natural gas, possible oil reserves, textiles, bananas, camels, cotton, goats, groundnuts, maize/corn, millet, sheep, sugarcane

SENEGAL

Senegal consists mostly of lowlying plains, with arid semidesert areas in the north and lush savanna and rain forest in the south, where along the coast are mangrove swamps. Senegal is a country with a strong artistic and literary tradition. Although the country is dependent on agriculture, with fishing also important, it has one of the largest manufacturing sectors in western Africa. Industries include food processing, construction, fertilizer production, petroleum refining, and textiles.

NATIONAL DATA – SENEGAL

Land area 192,000 sq km (74,132 sq mi)

| Climate | | Temperatures | Annual | |
	Altitude m (ft)	January °C(°F)	July °C(°F)	precipitation mm (in)
Dakar	23 (75)	22 (72)	26 (79)	514 (20.2)

Major physical features highest point: Futa Jalon (edge) 500 m (1,640 ft); longest river: Senegal (part) 1,633 km (1,015 mi)

Population (2006 est.) 11,987,121

Form of government Multiparty republic with one legislative house

Armed forces army 11,900; navy 950; air force 770

Capital city Dakar (2,564,900)

Official language French

Ethnic composition Wolof 43.3%; Pular 23.8%; Serer 14.7%; Jola 3.7%; Mandinka 3%; Soninke 1.1%; European and Lebanese 1%; other 9.4%

Religious affiliations Muslim 94%, Christian 5% (mainly Roman Catholic), traditional beliefs 1%

Currency 1 Communauté Financière Africaine franc (XOF) = 100 centimes

Gross domestic product (2006 est.) U.S. $22.01 billion

Gross domestic product per capita (2006 est.) U.S. $1,800

Life expectancy at birth male 57.7 yr; female 60.85 yr

Major resources fisheries, phosphates, iron ore, food processing, fertilizer production, petroleum refining, construction materials, textiles, groundnuts, maize/corn, millet, rice, sorghum; timber

GAMBIA

Tiny Gambia forms a narrow enclave along the banks and estuary of the swamp-lined Gambia River, surrounded on three sides by Senegal. The hills and plains support mainly savanna and forest, although much of the latter has been felled to make way for agriculture. Typical riverine species such as crocodiles, hippos, and waterbirds live in and around the river. The country depends on tourism, which accounts for over 50 percent of national income. The service industries, principally tourism and government-based activities, employ 67 percent of the workforce. Agricultural crops consist of groundnuts, palm kernels, cotton, millet, and rice. Commercial fishing is also well developed.

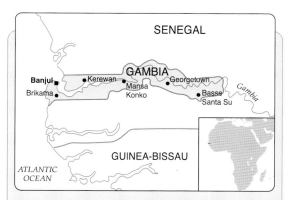

NATIONAL DATA – GAMBIA

Land area 10,000 sq km (3,861 sq mi)

| Climate | | Temperatures | | Annual |
	Altitude m (ft)	January °C(°F)	July °C(°F)	precipitation mm (in)
Banjul	2 (7)	24 (72)	27 (79)	977 (38.4)

Major physical features longest river: Gambia (part) 1,100 km (700 mi)

Population (2006 est.) 1,641,564

Form of government multiparty republic with one legislative house

Armed forces army 800

Capital city Banjul (34,828)

Official language English

Ethnic composition African 99% (Mandinka 42%; Fula 18%; Wolof 16%; Jola 10%; Serahuli 9%; other 4%); non-African 1%

Religious affiliations Muslim 90%; Christian 9%; traditional beliefs 1%

Currency 1 dalasi (GMD) = 100 butut

Gross domestic product (2006 est.) U.S. $3.25 billion

Gross domestic product per capita (2006 est.) U.S. $2,000

Life expectancy at birth male 52.3 yr; female 56.03 yr

Major resources fisheries, titanium (rutile and ilmenite), tin, zircon, silica sand, clay, petroleum, tourism, cassava, cattle, cotton, groundnuts, millet, palm kernels, rice, timber

GUINEA-BISSAU

Most of Guinea-Bissau is lowlying apart from upland savanna in the east. Mangrove swamps grow along the coast. The republic is the world's sixth largest exporter of cashew nuts, which are a major crop. Groundnuts (peanuts) and palm kernels are also produced commercially. About 80 percent of the labor force relies on subsistence farming, growing rice (the main food crop). Fishing has expanded in the last decade, and frozen shrimp and fish are exported. Offshore oil reserves have been found but have not yet been exploited. There are also unworked phosphate deposits.

NATIONAL DATA – GUINEA-BISSAU

Land area 28,000 sq km (10,811 sq mi)

Climate	Altitude m (ft)	Temperatures January °C(°F)	July °C(°F)	Annual precipitation mm (in)
Bissau	21 (69)	26 (78)	26 (78)	1,756 (69)

Population (2006 est.) 1,442,029

Form of government multiparty republic with one legislative house

Armed forces army 6,800; navy 350; air force 100

Capital city Bissau (420,412)

Official language Portuguese

Ethnic composition African 99% (includes Balanta 30%; Fula 20%; Manjaca 14%; Mandinga 13%; Papel 7%); European and mulatto 1%

Religious affiliations traditional beliefs 50%; Muslim 45%, Christian 5%

Currency 1 Communauté Financière Africaine franc (XOF) = 100 centimes

Gross domestic product (2006 est.) U.S. $1.244 billion

Gross domestic product per capita (2006 est.) U.S. $900

Life expectancy at birth male 45.05 yr; female 48.75 yr

Major resources fish, timber, bauxite, clay, granite, limestone, unexploited deposits of petroleum and phosphates, cashew nuts, groundnuts, palm kernels, rice, cereals, coconuts, cotton

GUINEA

Guinea's interior is mountainous and includes high savanna around the Niger River. The Guinea Highlands are covered in dense, tropical rain forests that yield hardwoods such as teak and ebony. There are mangrove swamps on the coast. Most of the workforce is employed in agriculture, although Guinea is the world's second largest producer of bauxite. Fighting in Sierra Leone and Liberia in the late 1990s caused an influx of half a million refugees into Guinea, disrupting the economy, stretching resources, and reducing foreign investment.

NATIONAL DATA – GUINEA

Land area 245,857 sq km (94,926 sq mi)

Climate	Altitude m (ft)	Temperatures January °C(°F)	July °C(°F)	Annual precipitation mm (in)
Conakry	46 (151)	26 (78)	25 (77)	3,805 (69)

Major physical features highest point: Mount Nimba 1,850 m (6,069 ft); longest river: Niger (part) 4,200 km (2,600 mi)

Population (2006 est.) 9,690,222

Form of government multiparty republic with one legislative assembly

Armed forces army 8,500; navy 400; air force 800

Largest cities Conakry (capital – 2,064,236); Nzerekore (138,862)

Official language French

Ethnic composition Peuhl 40%; Malinke 30%; Soussou 20%; other ethnic groups 10%

Religious affiliations Muslim 85%; Christian 8%; traditional beliefs 7%

Currency 1 Guinean franc (GNF) = 100 centimes

Gross domestic product (2006 est.) U.S. $19.4 billion

Gross domestic product per capita (2006 est.) U.S. $2,000

Life expectancy at birth male 48.34 yr; female 50.7 yr

Major resources bauxite, iron ore, diamonds, gold, uranium, hydropower, fish, salt, tropical fruits, timber

SIERRA LEONE

The landscape of Sierra Leone includes a coastline and many rivers lined with swamps, and heavily forested hills and mountains. The waterways are a main source of transport.

NATIONAL DATA – SIERRA LEONE

Land area 71,620 sq km (27,653 sq mi)

Climate	Altitude m (ft)	Temperatures January °C(°F)	July °C(°F)	Annual precipitation mm (in)
Freetown	11 (36)	27 (80)	26 (78)	2,946 (116)

Major physical features highest point: Bintimani Peak 1,948 m (6,391 ft)

Population (2006 est.) 6,005,250

Form of government multiparty republic with one legislative house

Armed forces joint forces 12–13,000

Capital city Freetown (835,108)

Official language English

Ethnic composition Native African tribes 90% (Temne 30%, Mende 30%, other 30%), Creole (Krio) 10%; small numbers of Europeans, Lebanese, Pakistanis, and Indians

Religious affiliations Muslim 60%; traditional beliefs 30%; Christian 10%

Currency 1 leone (SLL) = 100 cents

Gross domestic product (2006 est.) U.S. $5.38 billion

Gross domestic product per capita (2006 est.) U.S. $900

Life expectancy at birth male 38.05 yr; female 42.46 yr

Major resources diamonds, titanium ore, bauxite, iron ore, gold, chromite, cassava, cocoa, coffee, fish, groundnuts, palm nuts, rice, timber

Sierra Leone comprises a narrow coastal belt of mangrove swamps rising to an upland plateau of wood-clad hills and mountains and rolling savanna grassland. In the northeast the Loma Mountains rise to Bintimani Peak. The country is also crossed by many rivers that flow from across the Guinean border. The climate ranges from hot, tropical, and rainy, to dry and windy. In the 1990s civil war between the government and the Revolutionary United Front caused thousands of deaths and displaced about one-third of the population. An uneasy peace and civilian rule were restored in 2002. The country's progress is hampered by the unstable situations in Guinea and Liberia. Sierra Leone is very poor and relies on foreign aid.

About two-thirds of the people work on the land; palm kernels, cocoa, and coffee are the main cash crops, with rice the chief subsistence crop. Considerable farming and mining resources exist in the country, but the economic infrastructure is poorly developed and weak. Diamond mining is the major source of foreign currency earnings, although much of this commodity is smuggled out of the country. Manufacturing centers on Freetown and consists mostly of consumer goods.

LIBERIA

Africa's oldest independent republic, Liberia has a swamp-lined coast. Inland, rolling hills covered with tropical rain forest give way to a high plateau. There are mountains in the north. The UN has presided over a fragile ceasefire following the civil war which began in the 1990s, but war and government mismanagement have seriously damaged the country's economy. Many of the skilled people who could help recovery have fled abroad, and some 80 percent of the population lives below the poverty line. Rubber is the main cash crop, and most manufacturing serves only the local market.

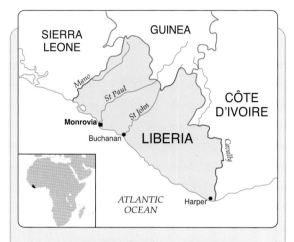

NATIONAL DATA – LIBERIA

Land area 96,320 sq km (37,189 sq mi)

Climate	Altitude m (ft)	Temperatures January °C(°F)	July °C(°F)	Annual precipitation mm (in)
Monrovia	23 (75)	27 (81)	25 (79)	5,140 (202.3)

Major physical features highest point: Mount Wutivi 1,380 m (4,528 ft); longest river: Cavally (part) 515 km (320 mi)

Population (2006 est.) 3,042,004

Form of government multiparty republic with two legislative houses

Armed forces Joint forces 15,000

Capital city Monrovia (967,841)

Official language English

Ethnic composition Indigenous African tribes 95% (including Kpelle, Bassa, Gio, Kru, Grebo, Mano, Krahn, Gola, Gbandi, Loma, Kissi, Vai, Dei, Bella, Mandingo, and Mende); Americo-Liberians (descendants of repatriated slaves) 5%

Religious affiliations traditional beliefs 40%; Christian 40%; Muslim 20%

Currency 1 Liberian dollar (LRD) = 100 cents

Gross domestic product (2006 est.) U.S. $2.911 billion

Gross domestic product per capita (2006 est.) U.S. $1,000

Life expectancy at birth male 37.99 yr; female 41.35 yr

Major resources iron ore, timber, diamonds, gold, hydropower, fish, rubber, cocoa, coffee, bananas, cassava, maize/corn, palm kernels, rice

CÔTE D'IVOIRE

Côte d'Ivoire consists mainly of flat or undulating plains, with highlands in the north. The northern plateau is covered with savanna, and four large rivers bisect the country. Much original rain forest has been felled for plantations. Following coups and civil war, peace-keeping forces are helping disarmament and reconciliation, but there is still tension between the north and the south, and the economy is damaged. The country is one of the world's largest coffee exporters, and yams, maize/corn, and rice are among the staple crops. Over 40 percent of Côte d'Ivoire's workforce is from abroad.

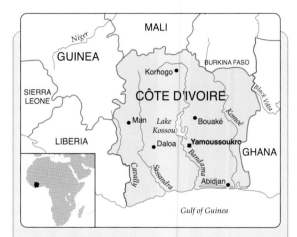

NATIONAL DATA – CÔTE D'IVOIRE

Land area 318,000 sq km (122, 780 sq mi)

Climate	Altitude m (ft)	Temperatures January °C(°F)	July °C(°F)	Annual precipitation mm (in)
Abidjan	7 (23)	27 (81)	26 (79)	1,959 (77.1)

Major physical features highest point: Mount Nimba 1,850 m (6,069 ft)

Population (2006 est.) 17,654,843

Form of government multiparty republic with one legislative house

Armed forces army 6,500; navy 900; air force 700

Largest cities Abidjan (3,918,000); Bouaké (597,507); Yamoussoukro (capital - 205,723)

Official language French

Ethnic composition Akan 42.1%; Voltaiques or Gur 17.6%; Northern Mandes 16.5%; Krous 11%; Southern Mandes 10%; other 2.8%

Religious affiliations Muslim 35–40%; traditional beliefs 25–40%; Christian 20–30%

Currency 1 Communauté Financière Africaine franc (XOF) = 100 centimes

Gross domestic product (2006 est.) U.S. $28.47 billion

Gross domestic product per capita (2006 est.) U.S. $1,600

Life expectancy at birth male 46.24 yr; female 51.48 yr

Major resources petroleum, natural gas, diamonds, manganese, iron ore, cobalt, bauxite, copper, gold, nickel, tantalum, silica sand, clay, cocoa beans, coffee, maize, palm oil, rice, yams, hydropower

BURKINA FASO

NATIONAL DATA – BURKINA FASO

Land area   273,800 sq km (105,715 sq mi)

Climate		Temperatures		Annual
	Altitude m (ft)	January °C(°F)	July °C(°F)	precipitation mm (in)
Abidjan	304 (997)	25 (77)	28 (79)	895 (35.2)

Major physical features   highest point: Téna Kouron 747 m (2,451 ft)

Population   (2006 est.) 13,902,972

Form of government   multiparty republic with two legislative houses

Armed forces   army 6,400; air force 200

Largest cities   Ouagadougou (capital - 1,152,402); Koudougou (91,468); Ouahigouya (63,598)

Official language   French

Ethnic composition   Mossi 47.9%; Mande 8.8%; Fulani 8.3%; Lobi 6.9%; Bobo 6.8%; Senufo 5.3%; Grosi 5.1%; Gurma 4.8%; Tuareg 3.3%; others 2.4%

Religious affiliations   Muslim 50%; traditional beliefs 40%; Christian (mainly Roman Catholic) 10%

Currency   1 Communauté Financière Africaine franc (XOF) = 100 centimes

Gross domestic product   (2006 est.) U.S. $17.87 billion

Gross domestic product per capita   (2006 est.) U.S. $1,300

Life expectancy at birth   male 47.33 yr; female 50.42 yr

Major resources   manganese, limestone, marble; small deposits of gold, phosphates, pumice, salt, antimony, bauxite, copper, cotton, groundnuts, lead, livestock, maize/corn, millet, nickel, rice, sesame, shea, sorghum, sugarcane

Bani, in northeastern Burkina Faso, is dominated by seven mosques. Each is elaborately constructed from baked mud-bricks and features Sudanese-style minarets.

Bordering the southern edge of the Sahara, most of Burkina Faso is a wide plateau with hills in the west. The three main rivers—the Red, White, and Black Voltas—cut deep valleys as they flow north to south. The scenery in the north is scrub and semidesert typical of the Sahel region, whereas the south has tropical savanna and forest. A series of coups followed independence from France in 1960, but multiparty elections were held in the early 1990s. However, an ongoing volatile political situation hampers progress toward stability.

Burkina Faso has few natural resources and a large population, resulting in poor economic prospects. Subsistence agriculture employs most of the people; cash crops include groundnuts, cotton (the main export), and sesame, while the main food crops are millet, sugarcane, and sorghum. Cattle and goats are raised in the north and east. Industry is undeveloped and is based mainly on agriculture. Employment opportunities in the country are low—over 2 million Burkinans work in neighboring Côte d'Ivoire and Ghana.

GHANA

Ghana was formerly known as the Gold Coast because 15th-century Portuguese explorers found alluvial gold there, washed down by the Volta River.

Geography

Most of Ghana is lowlying, so the hot tropical climate remains unmodified by altitude. Temperatures vary from season to season but are lowest near the coast, where sea mists have a cooling effect. The coastal vegetation of mangrove swamps rapidly gives way inland to savanna grassland and then to tropical forest, which covers the southern third of the country—although much of it has been cleared for agriculture. More than half of the country is occupied by the Volta Basin—a fertile, often flooded area surrounding the massive and elongated Lake Volta, which was itself created by the construction of the Akosombo Dam. The Volta River eventually flows into a series of coastal lagoons and marshes. Ghana is relatively rich in wildlife, including big cats such as lions and leopards, elephants, antelopes, crocodiles, and manatees. The largest of several game reserves is the Mole, near Damongo in the northwest.

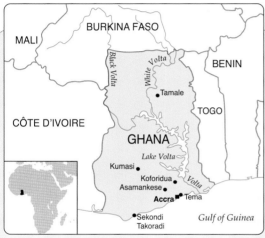

NATIONAL DATA – GHANA

Land area   230,940 sq km (89,166 sq mi)

Climate	Altitude m (ft)	Temperatures January °C(°F)	July °C(°F)	Annual precipitation mm (in)
Accra	65 (213)	27 (81)	25 (77)	725 (28.5)

Major physical features   highest point: Mount Afadjoto 885 m (2,903 ft); largest lake: Lake Volta 8,482 sq km (3,275 sq mi)

Population   (2006 est.) 22,409,572

Form of government   republic with multiparty parliament

Armed forces   army 5,000; navy 1,000; air force 1,000

Largest cities   Accra (capital – 2,096,653); Kumasi (1,604,909); Tamale (390,730); Takoradi (260,651); Ashiaman (228,509); Tema (161,106)

Official language   English

Ethnic composition   Black African 98.5% (major tribes – Akan 44%; Moshi-Dagomba 16%; Ewe 13%; Ga 8%; Gurma 3%; Yoruba 1%); other 1.5%

Religious affiliations   Christian 63%; Muslim 16%; traditional beliefs 21%

Currency   1 cedi (GHC) = 100 pesewas

Gross domestic product   (2006 est.) U.S. $59.15 billion

Gross domestic product per capita   (2006 est.) U.S. $2,600

Life expectancy at birth   male 58.07 yr; female 59.69 yr

Major resources   gold, timber, industrial diamonds, bauxite, manganese, fish, rubber, hydropower, petroleum, natural gas, silver, salt, limestone, bananas, cassava, cocoa, maize/corn, sorghum, taro, yams, tourism

Society

Ghana's interior has been settled by many ethnic groups, including the Ashanti who were dominant by the 17th century. The Portuguese were also influential in the area, but by the 19th century the British took control. By 1901 the Gold Coast was a British colony, and after World War I part of neighboring Togoland also came under British control. Today Ghana has some 75 ethnic groups, although only 10 are of significant size—the largest being the Akan and the Mossi.

A Ghanaian fishing port. Both marine and freshwater fishing are encouraged as an important way of supplementing the diet.

Economy

Ghana is rich in natural resources such as oil, diamonds, gold, and timber. The country has nearly double the per capita output of many other West African countries, but despite this, Ghana still relies on foreign financial and technical support to help its economy.

Most people (about 60 percent) are employed in subsistence and smallholding agriculture, which is the mainstay of the economy. Cocoa and timber are the chief export crops. Yams and cereals are grown in the north, and cattle are raised, while the forests produce shea and kola nuts. Despite government efforts to increase food production, Ghana still imports food. Gold is a key export, and diamonds, manganese, and bauxite are also important. Oil and natural gas are also exported. However, several of Ghana's chief exports, such as cocoa and gold, are highly susceptible to fluctuating markets. Hydroelectric power from the Akosombo Dam supplies domestic needs, with the surplus being exported. Manufacturing is limited mainly to supplying local demand. Tourism is increasing. Road and rail transportation is best developed in the south, particularly in the cocoa-growing areas around the coast. About a quarter of roads are paved, and the rail system is chiefly used to transport freight.

Healthcare has been hindered by rapid population growth, bad sanitation, and poor nutrition. Some major diseases have been partly controlled, but infant mortality is high, and life expectancy is relatively short.

GHANA SINCE INDEPENDENCE

In 1957 the newly renamed state of Ghana was the first sub-Saharan country in colonial Africa to win independence, and in 1960 it was declared a republic. Successive coups followed, resulting in the suspension of the constitution in 1981 and a ban on political parties. Multiparty politics was restored in 1992, and a new constitution approved. Flight Lieutenant Jerry Rawlings (b. 1947) became head of state in 1981 and won elections in 1992 and 1996. Under the constitution he was not allowed to run for a third term, and he stepped down in 2000 when John Kufuor (b. 1938) became president.

TOGO

Togo extends through southern coastal lagoons on the Bight of Benin via plateaus and forested hills to savanna in the north, where it borders Burkina Faso. Togo has been dogged by coups, violence, and a perceived lack of democracy since independence, which have discouraged foreign investment. Cotton is the most important cash crop, and cattle, sheep, and pigs are raised in the north. However, the country's most important asset is phosphates, accounting for half of all exports. Other industries include food processing, cement, textiles, beverages, and handicrafts.

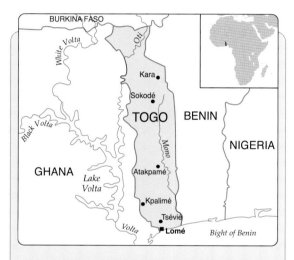

NATIONAL DATA – TOGO

Land area	54,385 sq km (20,998 sq mi)			
Climate		Temperatures		Annual
	Altitude m (ft)	January °C(°F)	July °C(°F)	precipitation mm (in)
Lomé	20 (66)	27 (81)	25 (77)	1,577 (62)

Major physical features highest point: Pic Baumann 986 m (3,235 ft); longest river: Mono 400 km (250 mi)
Population (2006 est.) 5,548,702
Form of government Republic under transition to multiparty democratic rule
Armed forces army 8,100; navy 200; air force 250
Capital city Lomé (756,122)
Official language French
Ethnic composition Native African (37 tribes; largest are Ewe, Mina, and Kabre) 99%; European and Syrian-Lebanese less than 1%
Religious affiliations traditional beliefs 51%; Christian 29%; Muslim 20%
Currency 1 Communauté Financière Africaine franc (XOF) = 100 centimes
Gross domestic product (2006 est.) U.S. $9.248 billion
Gross domestic product per capita (2006 est.) U.S. $1,700
Life expectancy at birth male 55.41 yr; female 59.49 yr
Major resources phosphates, limestone, marble, livestock, food processing, cement, textiles, beverages, handicrafts, coffee, copra, cocoa, cotton

BENIN

From the coast Benin's land rises to a fertile, heavily cultivated plateau with some hills and low mountains. The northern region is covered with forest and savanna, inhabited by wildlife. The centrally planned economy has now been dismantled in favor of the free market and public utilities have been privatized, although the economy relies heavily on foreign aid. Half the population depends on agriculture—many as subsistence farmers—with cotton and coffee among the cash crops.

NATIONAL DATA – BENIN

Land area	110,620 sq km (42,710 sq mi)			
Climate		Temperatures		Annual
	Altitude m (ft)	January °C(°F)	July °C(°F)	precipitation mm (in)
Cotonou	5 (16)	27 (81)	26 (79)	1,308 (51.4)

Major physical features highest point: Atakora Massif 641 m (2,103 ft)
Population (2006 est.) 7,862,944
Form of government multiparty republic with one legislative house
Armed forces army 4,300; navy 100; air force 150
Largest cities Cotonou (711,600); Abomey-Calavi (443,670); Porto Novo (capital – 242,187); Djougou (217,360)
Official language French
Ethnic composition African 99% (42 ethnic groups, largest are Fon, Adja, Yoruba, Bariba); Europeans 5,500
Religious affiliations traditional beliefs 50%; Christian 30%; Muslim 20%
Currency 1 Communauté Financière Africaine franc (XOF) = 100 centimes
Gross domestic product (2006 est.) U.S. $8.931 billion
Gross domestic product per capita (2006 est.) U.S. $1,100
Life expectancy at birth male 51.9 yr; female 54.22 yr
Major resources small offshore oil deposits, limestone (cement), marble, timber, beans, cassava, coffee, cotton, groundnuts, maize/corn, palm products, sorghum, yams

SÃO TOMÉ AND PRÍNCIPE

The smallest country in Africa, São Tomé and Príncipe is a group of volcanic mountainous islands in the Gulf of Guinea. São Tomé, clad in rain forest, was formerly a settlement for convicts banished to the island by the Portuguese. Since independence the islands have seen a Marxist system of government, a multiparty democratic system, and attempted coups. Cocoa has been the mainstay of this poor nation's economy since independence, but production has suffered through drought and mismanagement. About one-third of the land is cultivated for export crops, so staples are mostly imported. There is scope for tourism in the future.

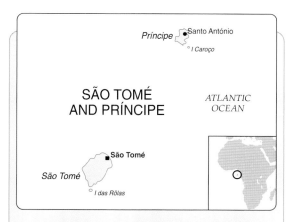

NATIONAL DATA – SÃO TOMÉ AND PRÍNCIPE

Land area   1,001 sq km (386 sq mi)

Climate	Altitude m (ft)	Temperatures January °C(°F)	July °C(°F)	Annual precipitation mm (in)
São Tomé	8 (26)	27 (81)	25 (77)	966 (38.1)

Major physical features   highest point: Pico de Tomé 2,024 m (6,640 ft); largest island: São Tomé 855 sq km (332 sq mi)

Population   (2006 est.) 193,413

Form of government   multiparty republic with two legislative houses

Armed forces   no armed forces

Capital city   São Tomé (65,416)

Official language   Portuguese

Ethnic composition   African (mainly Fang) 90%; Portuguese and Creole 10%

Religious affiliations   Catholic 70.3%; Evangelical 3.4%; New Apostolic 2%; Adventist 1.8%; other 3.1%; none 19.4%

Currency   1 dobra (STD) = 100 cêntimos

Gross domestic product   (2003 est.) U.S. $214 million

Gross domestic product per capita   (2003 est.) U.S. $1,200

Life expectancy at birth   male 65.73 yr; female 68.95 yr

Major resources   cocoa, copra, coffee, bananas, palm oil, fisheries, tourism, fish, hydropower, coconuts, timber

CAPE VERDE

Cape Verde is a group of 10 islands and five islets in two archipelagos west of Senegal. Most have sandy beaches, but inland the terrain is mountainous. Fogo has an active volcano. Cape Verde is an important sea and air refueling site, and one of Africa's more stable democracies. Agriculture is only possible where sea mists linger, and service industries account for 70 percent of GDP. Natural resources, including water, are scant, and much foreign aid has been spent on projects such as water conservation. Money sent back from Cape Verdeans working abroad is vital to the economy.

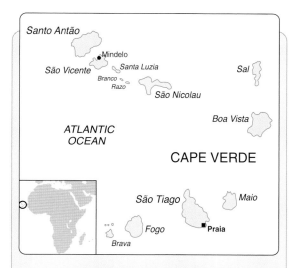

NATIONAL DATA – CAPE VERDE

Land area   4,033 sq km (159 sq mi)

Climate	Altitude m (ft)	Temperatures January °C(°F)	July °C(°F)	Annual precipitation mm (in)
Praia	27 (89)	23 (73)	26 (79)	2,172 (85.5)

Major physical features   highest point: Pico do Cano (Fogo) 2,829 m (9,281 ft); largest island: São Tiago 991 sq km (383 sq mi)

Population   (2006 est.) 420,979

Form of government   multiparty republic with one legislative house

Armed forces   army 1.000; coast guard 100; air force 100

Capital city   Praia (121,393)

Official language   Portuguese

Ethnic composition   Creole (mulatto) 71%; African 28%; European 1%

Religious affiliations   Roman Catholic 97.8%; others 2.2%

Currency   1 Cape Verdean escudo (CVE) = 100 centavos

Gross domestic product   (2006 est.) U.S. $3.129 billion

Gross domestic product per capita   (2006 est.) U.S. $6,000

Life expectancy at birth   male 67.41 yr; female 74.15 yr

Major resources   salt, basalt rock, limestone, kaolin, fisheries, clay, gypsum, bananas, coffee, coconuts

Nigeria is the most highly populated country on the African continent and one of the most influential. Its diverse culture is the result of its many different peoples—more than 200—but interethnic rivalries, often violent, have been a way of life since the country gained independence in 1960. Compared with many African countries Nigeria is a modern and prosperous nation.

NATIONAL DATA – NIGERIA

Land area	910,768 sq km (351,649 sq mi)			
Climate		**Temperatures**		**Annual precipitation**
	Altitude m (ft)	January °C(°F)	July °C(°F)	mm (in)
Lagos	3 (10)	27 (81)	2 (77)	1,538 (60.5)

Major physical features highest point: Dimiong 2,042 m (6,700 ft); longest river: Niger (part) 4,200 km (2,600 mi)
Population (2006 est.) 131,859,731
Form of government federal republic with military government
Armed forces army 62,000; navy 7,000; air force 9,500
Largest cities Lagos (9,229,944); Kano (3,848,885); Ibadan (3,847,472); Kaduna (1,652,844); Abuja (capital since 1991 – 1,405,201)
Official language English
Ethnic composition Hausa 21.3%; Yoruba 21.3%; Ibo 18.0%; Fulani 11.2%; Ibibio 5.6%; Kanuri 4.2%; Edo 3.4%; Tiv 2.2%; Ijaw 1.8%; Bura 1.7%; Nupe 1.2%; others 8.1%
Religious affiliations Muslim 50%; Christian 40%; traditional beliefs or none 10%
Currency 1 naira (NGN) = 100 kobo
Gross domestic product (2006 est.) U.S. $188.5 billion
Gross domestic product per capita (2006 est.) U.S. $1,400
Life expectancy at birth male 46.52 yr; female 47.66 yr
Major resources natural gas, petroleum, tin, iron ore, lead, zinc, coal, fisheries, palm kernels, cassava, cocoa, cotton, groundnuts, livestock, maize/corn, millet, rice, rubber, sorghum, timber, yams

Geography

The southern third of the country consists of humid forested lowlands. Progressing north, the terrain becomes drier, with hills and plateaus, and the vegetation more savannalike. The Jos Plateau lies at the heart of Nigeria, and from it the land falls away to the Niger border. The Yankari National Park, east of Jos, is West Africa's best nature reserve and a refuge for wildlife including elephants, waterbuck, hippos, lions, and crocodiles. The northern third of the country forms part of the semiarid Sahel region on the edges of the Sahara. The mountain chains along the eastern border are a continuation of the Adamawa Highlands. The Niger and Benue Rivers divide Nigeria roughly into three as they flow from northeast and northwest before meeting and then sweeping south through tropical rain forests and swamps to empty into the Gulf of Guinea at the vast Niger Delta. In many places the rain forest, with its hardwood trees such as iroko and mahogany, has been cleared for cultivation. The tropical climate is varied: in the north it is hot and often arid, whereas near the coast it is humid with high rainfall.

Society

There were many ancient city-states in Nigeria, including the Yoruba city of Ife, the mainly Hausa Kanem-Bornu kingdom, and the Benin kingdom in the southwest. The legacy of these empires includes highly crafted works in ivory, wood, bronze, and brass—for example, those of Ife and Benin. In 1960 Nigeria gained independence from Britain as a federal state made up of four regions. In 1961 the northern half of British Cameroon joined the federation. Today, Hausa and Fulanis dominate the north, with the Yoruba, Edo, and Ibo making up the largest groups in the south.

Economy

Compared with most African countries Nigeria has a fairly well-developed transportation system, including roads, railroads, inland waterways, and ports. It also has a good general infrastructure, although telecommunications are erratic and power supplies are subject to failure without warning. Much of the country is also fertile, and there are plentiful natural resources,

particularly petroleum, coal, and iron ore. Nevertheless, many of the people still live in traditional villages and work the land. Cocoa and rubber, the chief export crops, are grown mainly in the south, and palm kernels mainly in the east. The main staples are cassava, yams, rice, millet, and sorghum. However, subsistence agriculture has not been able to feed the rapidly growing population, and the country, once a large net exporter of food, now imports food. Nigeria is rich in minerals such as coal, iron ore, oil, zinc, and lead; oil provides 95 percent of foreign exchange earnings. Much of the revenue from Nigeria's petroleum has been squandered through mismanagement, corruption, and political instability, and despite its rich natural reserves Nigeria is one of the most indebted of all African countries. Manufacturing industries include paper products, cement, cigarettes, and various consumer goods.

The southern third of Nigeria consists of dense, humid forested and wooded lowlands, still rich in wildlife in many places.

THE NIGERIAN CIVIL WAR

In 1966 Ibo army officers seized the government in a coup. This led to the massacre of thousands of Ibo in the Northern Region. Following a Hausa countercoup, Lieutenant-Colonel Yakubu Gowon (b. 1934) was made president and worked for reconciliation. But in 1967 the Ibo-dominated Eastern Region seceded as the state of Biafra under Lieutenant-Colonel C. Odumegwu Ojukwu (b. 1933). After a bloody war in which many Ibo died, Biafra collapsed in 1970. Gowon refrained from making reprisals, but for many years military coups thwarted attempts to restore a stable civilian government.

CAMEROON

Cameroon is mainly rain-forest-clad plateaus rising to highlands and then sloping down to Lake Chad in the north. Mount Cameroon is an active volcano. The diversity of Cameroon's agriculture and the rapid development of the petroleum industry (making oil the largest export), have given the country many advantages, but Cameroon is still underdeveloped and one of the world's most indebted nations. The climate for business is hampered by a top-heavy state sector.

NATIONAL DATA –CAMEROON

Land area	469,440 sq km (181,252 sq mi)			
Climate		Temperatures		Annual precipitation
	Altitude m (ft)	January °C(°F)	July °C(°F)	mm (in)
Yaoundé	760 (2,493)	24 (75)	23 (73)	657 (25.9)

Major physical features highest point: Mount Cameroon 4,070 m (13,353 ft)	
Population (2006 est.) 17,340,702	
Form of government multiparty republic with one legislative house	
Armed forces army 12.500; navy 1,300; air force 300	
Largest cities Douala (1,404,831); Yaoundé (capital – 1,390,516)	
Official languages French, English	
Ethnic composition Cameroon Highlanders 31%; Equatorial Bantu 19%; Kirdi 11%; Fulani 10%; Northwestern Bantu 8%; Eastern Nigritic 7%; other African 13%; non-African 1%	
Religious affiliations traditional beliefs 40%; Christian 40%; Muslim 20%	
Currency 1 Communauté Financière Africaine franc (XAF) = 100 centimes	
Gross domestic product (2006 est.) U.S. $42.2 billion	
Gross domestic product per capita (2006 est.) U.S. $2,400	
Life expectancy at birth male 50.98 yr; female 51.34 yr	
Major resources petroleum, bauxite, iron ore, hydropower, cocoa, cassava, coffee, cotton, groundnuts, gold, livestock, maize, millet, natural gas, palm oil, plantains, rubber, sorghum, sweet potatoes, timber, tin, yams	

CENTRAL AFRICAN REPUBLIC

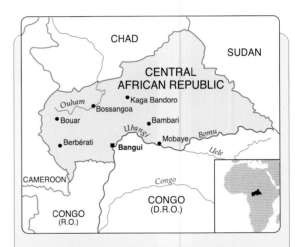

Most of this landlocked country consists of an undulating plateau flanked by uplands in the northeast and west. The climate ranges from near-desert in the far north to lush equatorial in the south. Here the dense rain forest is one of the last strongholds of the Lowland Gorilla. Subsistence agriculture forms the backbone of the economy, with groundnuts and cotton among the crops raised for export. Diamonds are the Republic's main natural resource. Manufacturing is small scale.

NATIONAL DATA – CENTRAL AFRICAN REPUBLIC

Land area	622,984 sq km (240,535 sq mi)			
Climate		Temperatures		Annual precipitation
	Altitude m (ft)	January °C(°F)	July °C(°F)	mm (in)
Bangui	381 (1,250)	26 (79)	25 (77)	1,545 (60.8)

Major physical features highest point: Kayagangiri 1,420 m (4,660 ft)	
Population (2006 est.) 4,303,356	
Form of government multiparty republic with one legislative house	
Armed forces army 1,400; air force 150	
Capital city Bangui (552,904)	
Official languages French, Sango	
Ethnic composition Baya 33%; Banda 27%; Mandjia 13%; Sara 10%; Mboum 7%; M'Baka 4%; Yakoma 4%; other 2%	
Religious affiliations traditional beliefs 35%; Protestant 25%; Roman Catholic 25%; Muslim 15%	
Currency 1 Communauté Financière Africaine franc (XAF) = 100 centimes	
Gross domestic product (2006 est.) U.S. $4.913 billion	
Gross domestic product per capita (2006 est.) U.S. $1,100	
Life expectancy at birth male 43.46 yr; female 43.62 yr	
Major resources diamonds, uranium, timber, gold, oil, hydropower, bananas, cassava, coffee, cotton, groundnuts, livestock, maize/corn, millet, plantains, sweet potatoes	

EQUATORIAL GUINEA

The mainland rises from a narrow coastal plain to inland plateaus and hills, half of which are cloaked in forest, and rich in wildlife. The equatorial climate is hot and humid, with two rainy seasons. Subsistence agriculture supports about 75 percent of the population. Food processing is the only industry. Oil production is very important to the economy, and the country is Africa's third largest exporter of oil. There are also unexploited reserves of various minerals. Corruption is rife within Equatorial Guinea, and this has led to the suspension of international aid packages.

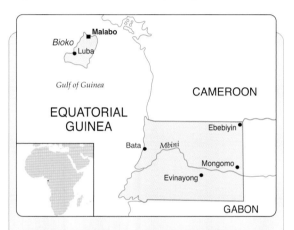

NATIONAL DATA – EQUATORIAL GUINEA

Land area	28,051 sq km (10,831 sq mi)			
Climate		**Temperatures**		**Annual precipitation**
	Altitude m (ft)	January °C(°F)	July °C(°F)	mm (in)
Malabo	50 (164)	25 (77)	25 (77)	1,799 (70.8)

Major physical features highest point: Pico de Santa Isabel 3,007 m (9,685 ft); largest island: Bioko 2,017 sq km (779 sq mi)
Population (2006 est.) 540,109
Form of government multiparty republic but ruled more as a dictatorship
Armed forces army 1,100; navy 120; air force 100
Capital city Malabo (166,535)
Official languages Spanish, French
Ethnic composition Fang 72.0%; Bubi 14.7%; Duala 2.7%; Ibibio 1.3%; Maka 1.3%; others 8.0%
Religious affiliations Roman Catholic 88.8%; traditional beliefs 4.6%; Muslim 0.5%; others 0.2%; none 5.9%
Currency 1 Communauté Financière Africaine franc (XAF) = 100 centimes
Gross domestic product (2005 est.) U.S. $25.69 billion
Gross domestic product per capita (2006 est.) U.S. $6,572
Life expectancy at birth male 48 yr; female 51.13 yr
Major resources petroleum, natural gas, timber, gold, bauxite, diamonds, tantalum, sand, gravel, clay, bananas, cassava, cocoa, coconuts, coffee, sweet potatoes

GABON

The Ogooué River runs through the center of Gabon, cutting deep valleys through the country's uneven plateaus before forming a wide coastal delta. Dense rain forest covers most of the country. Almost half the population lives in Libreville, the capital. Agriculture is mostly in the from of subsistence farming, but it is Gabon's mineral reserves that have contributed most to the country's prosperity. Although there has been a decline in poverty, great inequalities in wealth exist.

NATIONAL DATA – GABON

Land area	257,667 sq km (99,486 sq mi)			
Climate		**Temperatures**		**Annual precipitation**
	Altitude m (ft)	January °C(°F)	July °C(°F)	mm (in)
Libreville	9 (30)	27 (81)	24 (75)	2,509 (98.7)

Major physical features highest point: Mont Milondo 1,020 m (3,346 ft)
Population (2006 est.) 1,424,906
Form of government multiparty republic with one legislative house
Armed forces army 3,200; navy 500; air force 1,000
Capital city Libreville (604,265)
Official language French
Ethnic composition Fang 35.5%; Mpongwe 15.1%; Mbete 14.2%; Punu 1.5%; others 23.7%
Religious affiliations Roman Catholic 65.2%; Protestant 18.8%; African Christian 12.1%; traditional beliefs 2.9%; Muslim 0.8%; others 0.2%
Currency 1 Communauté Financière Africaine franc (XAF) = 100 centimes
Gross domestic product (2006 est.) U.S. $10.21 billion
Gross domestic product per capita (2006 est.) U.S. $7,200
Life expectancy at birth male 53.21 yr; female 55.81 yr
Major resources petroleum, natural gas, diamonds, niobium, manganese, uranium, gold, timber, iron ore, hydropower, bananas, cassava, cocoa, coffee, livestock, maize/corn, palm oil, plantains, rice, sugarcane

Straddling the equator in the heart of the African continent, the Democratic Republic of the Congo (formerly known as Zaire) is bordered by nine other African nations. Almost landlocked, apart from a 50-km (30-mi) strip of coastline, the country is the third largest in Africa after Algeria and Sudan.

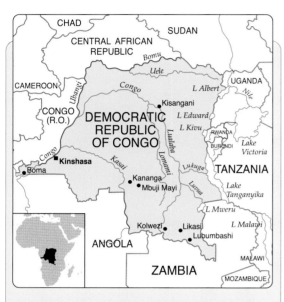

NATIONAL DATA – CONGO (D.R.O.)

Land area 2,267,600 sq km (875,525 sq mi)

Climate	Altitude m (ft)	Temperatures January °C(°F)	July °C(°F)	Annual precipitation mm (in)
Kinshasa	311 (1,020)	26 (79)	23 (73)	1,358 (53.4)

Major physical features highest point: Mount Stanley 5,109 m (16,763 ft); largest lake: :Lake Tanganyika (part) 32,900 sq km (12,700 sq mi)

Population (2006 est.) 62,660,551

Form of government transitional multiparty republic

Armed forces army 60,000; navy 1,800; air force 3,000

Capital city Kinshasa (8,418,819)

Official language French

Ethnic composition Luba 18.0%; Kongo 16.1%; Mongo 13.5%; Rwanda 10.3%; Azande 6.1%; Bangi/Ngale 5.8%; Rundi 3.8%; Teke 2.7%; Boa 2.3%; Chokwe 1.8%; Lugbara 1.6%; Banda 1.4%; others 16.6%

Religious affiliations Roman Catholic 50%; Protestant 20%; Kimbanguist 10%; Muslim 10%; other syncretic sects and traditional beliefs 10%

Currency 1 Congo franc (CDF) = 100 centimes

Gross domestic product (2006 est.) U.S. $44.6 billion

Gross domestic product per capita (2006 est.) U.S. $700

Life expectancy at birth male 50.01 yr; female 52.94 yr

Major resources cobalt, copper, niobium, tantalum, petroleum, industrial and gem diamonds, gold, silver, zinc, manganese, tin, uranium, coal, hydropower, timber, bananas, cassava, cocoa, coffee, cotton, groundnuts, maize/corn, millet, natural gas, plantains, palm oil and kernels, rice, rubber, sugarcane, tea

Geography

The huge Congo River rises in the west and flows north and west in a great horseshoe shape, meeting the Ubangi River on the Congo (Republic of) border. The vast Congo Basin occupies central and northwestern Congo, surrounded by higher plateau country. This becomes mountainous along the eastern border, where the Great Rift Valley is marked by lakes such as Lake Tanganyika and by many ranges of volcanic mountains. To the south rise the peaks of the Shaba Plateau. To the west the Congo River runs between more plateaus before entering the Atlantic Ocean.

In addition to the vast swamplands, the Congo Basin contains one of the world's greatest expanses of tropical rain forest, nurtured by frequent heavy rainfall and consistently high temperatures. The rain forest is one of the last refuges for rare and endangered animals such as the okapi and the Mountain Gorilla. Their future is by no means secure, since huge areas of the rain forest are fast disappearing as a result of felling. In the

Masked drummers, dancers, and a stilt walker of the Chokwe performing at a festival. One of the country's many ethnic groups, Chokwe people make up less than 2 percent of the population.

east and south of the country the forests give way to savanna woodlands and grasslands, supported by heavy seasonal rainfall. Wildlife in these areas includes giraffes, lions, antelopes, and the endangered black and white rhinoceroses. National parks have been set up in an attempt to conserve the wildlife, although the present political climate is not conducive to a focus on conservation issues.

Society

The Democratic Republic of the Congo is home to more than 200 ethnic groups, mostly Bantu. Many of them had created their own kingdoms before the Europeans arrived in the 19th century. The region's recent history has been difficult: early Belgian possession was initially marked by exploitation as well as atrocities carried out by concessionary companies; postcolonial events have been notable for ongoing anarchy, assassinations,

THE COUNTRY'S CHANGING NAME

King Leopold of Belgium (1835–1909) established the so-called Congo Free State and ran it as his own domain until he was forced to grant proper colonial status to the area in 1908, calling it the Belgian Congo. After independence as the Republic of the Congo (also known as Congo-Leopoldville) in 1960, army mutinies followed, and in 1965 Joseph-Désiré Mobutu (1930–97) seized power. He changed the country's name to Zaire. In 1997 Mobutu was ousted by rebel forces led by Laurent Kabila (1939–2001). He declared himself president, renaming the country the Democratic Republic of the Congo.

massive corruption, civil war, and foreign-backed insurrections. Further problems were caused by an influx of Rwandan refugees. Since 2003, Joseph Kabila (b. 1971) has headed a transitional government which also includes former rebels and members of the political opposition. However, despite the delicate ceasefire brought about by the Pretoria Accord, the government is only in full control of pockets of the country around the major cities.

Economy

Civil war has had a serious impact on the economy. Although the country's agriculture is potentially rich, apart from some large plantations it remains mostly at the subsistence level. Cash crops include coffee, cocoa, rubber, and cotton. The main staple crops are cassava, maize/corn, rice, and millet. The Democratic Republic of the Congo has great mineral wealth: a major copper belt extends across the southern border, the deposits of cobalt in the region are among the world's largest, and the country produces over half the world's low-grade industrial diamonds. There are also petroleum reserves off the coast. Ore smelting and petroleum refining are the main industries. Despite these riches, the wars and corruption (especially under Mobutu) meant that profits from industry were not used for development between 1965 and 1997. Furthermore, infrastructure such as roads has declined in the last 50 years. The country is now one of the four most heavily indebted in the world.

The Republic of Congo is a strip of land that extends into the heart of Africa from the western Atlantic coast.

Geography

The narrow coastal plain runs between neighboring Gabon and the Angolan enclave of Cabinda. Immediately inland are the Massif du Mayombé and the Niari Valley. Farther east the land rises again to a series of plateaus that form the western rim of the great Congo River Basin. This covers the northeast of the country, an area crisscrossed by rivers and swamps.

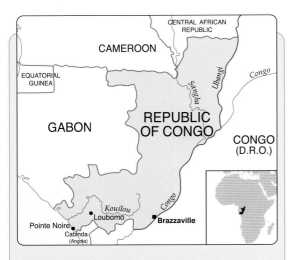

NATIONAL DATA – CONGO (R.O.)

Land area 341,500 sq km (131,854 sq mi)

Climate	Altitude m (ft)	Temperatures January °C(°F)	July °C(°F)	Annual precipitation mm (in)
Brazzaville	314 (1,030)	26 (79)	23 (73)	1,493 (58.7)

Major physical features highest point: Monts de la Lékéti 1,040 m (3,410 ft); longest river: Congo (part) 4,630 km (2,880 mi)

Population (2006 est.) 3,702,314

Form of government multiparty republic with one legislative house

Armed forces army 8,000; navy 800; air force 1,200

Largest cities Brazzaville (capital – 1,370,612); Pointe Noire (708,772)

Official language French

Ethnic composition Kongo 48%; Sangha 20%; M'Bochi 12%; Teke 17%; other 3%

Religious affiliations Christian 50%; animist 48%; Muslim 2%

Currency 1 Communauté Financière Africaine franc (XAF) = 100 centimes

Gross domestic product (2006 est.) U.S. $4.958 billion

Gross domestic product per capita (2006 est.) U.S. $1,300

Life expectancy at birth male 51.65 yr; female 53.98 yr

Major resources petroleum, timber, potash, lead, zinc, uranium, copper, phosphates, gold, magnesium, natural gas, hydropower, bananas, cassava, cocoa, coffee, groundnuts, palm oil, rice, sugarcane, sweet potatoes

The Congo River and its great tributary, the Ubangi, mark Congo's eastern border. The country's climate is tropical throughout, but rainfall varies according to latitude. The east has savanna grassland supporting animals such as giraffes and rhinos, but most of the country is covered with dense rain forest, inhabited by animals such as buffaloes, okapi, and gorillas.

Society

The forests of the Congo Basin were first settled by Mbuti, Twa, and Mbenga peoples. They were followed by Kongo peoples. In 1891 the region became the French Congo. The country was harshly exploited by concessionary companies until the 1930s. After independence in 1960 Fulbert Youlou (1917–72) became first president of the newly formed Republic of Congo (also known as Congo-Brazzaville). His overthrow in 1963 was followed by nearly 25 years of experimentation with Marxism. This was abandoned in 1990, and a democratically elected government was installed in 1992. A brief civil war in 1997 restored former Marxist president Sassou-Nguesso (b. 1943), but unrest followed. Southern-based rebels agreed to a final peace accord in 2003. About 70 percent of the population—a mix of diverse tribal groups—lives in Brazzaville and in Pointe Noire, or along the railroad in between.

Economy

The agricultural sector consists mainly of low-yield subsistence farming of wheat, maize/corn, plantains, cassava, and yams. Cocoa and coffee are grown for export. About 60 percent of the country is covered in tropical forest—half of which can be exploited economically—and forestry, particularly in the southern regions, has contributed significantly to the economy. However, the country's major resource is now oil, which accounts for 90 percent of export revenues and 70 percent of government revenue. Congo relies on imports of food and other items such as machinery, transportation equipment, chemicals, iron, and steel. Most of these are provided by France. The country's industrial base and infrastructure (and therefore also the economy) have been blighted by the civil war, political instability, and poor debt management.

RWANDA

Landlocked Rwanda is dominated in the west by Lake Kivu. To the east the land rises steeply to the mountains of the Congo–Nile divide. In the east there are plateaus with woods and savanna grassland. Ongoing disputes between the Tutsi and the Hutu peoples erupted into civil war in 1990, culminating in 1994 in a genocide during which about 1 million Tutsis and moderate Hutus were killed. Despite international aid and elections, the country has not resolved its political or economic problems. The economy, based on agriculture, has been seriously damaged.

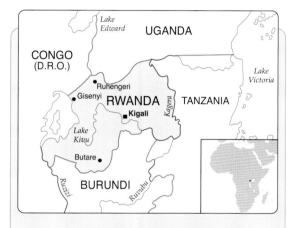

NATIONAL DATA – RWANDA

Land area 24,948 sq km (9,632 sq mi)

Climate	Altitude m (ft)	Temperatures January °C(°F)	July °C(°F)	Annual precipitation mm (in)
Kigali	1,545 (5,069)	19 (67)	21 (70)	1,028 (40.4)

Major physical features highest point: Mount Karisimbi 4,507 m (14,787 ft); largest lake: Lake Kivu (part) 2,699 sq km (1,042 sq mi)

Population (2006 est.) 8,648,248

Form of government presidential multiparty republic. New Constitution adopted in 2003.

Armed forces army 40,000; air force 1,000

Capital city Kigali (857,719)

Official languages Kinyarwanda, French, English

Ethnic composition Hutu 84%; Tutsi 15%; Twa (Pygmoid) 1%

Religious affiliations Roman Catholic 56.5%; Protestant 26%; Adventist 11.1%; Muslim 4.6%; traditional beliefs 0.1%; none 1.7%

Currency 1 Rwandan franc (RWF) = 100 centimes

Gross domestic product (2006) U.S. $13.54 billion

Gross domestic product per capita (2006) U.S. $1,600

Life expectancy at birth male 46.26 yr; female 48.38 yr

Major resources gold, cassiterite (tin ore), wolframite (tungsten ore), methane, hydropower, coffee, tea, sugarcane, bananas, beans and peas, cassava, cattle, groundnuts, goats, potatoes, pyrethrum, pigs, sheep, sorghum, sweet potatoes

BURUNDI

Along Burundi's western border the land is mountainous, with some areas still forested. Toward the east the land forms an irregular, savanna-clad plateau bisected by the Ruvubu River. Densely populated Burundi has suffered from political and ethnic unrest between Hutus and Tutsi peoples for decades, displacing or killing hundreds of thousands. A South African-brokered ceasefire is in place, but it faces many challenges. Burundi is poorly resourced with an underdeveloped manufacturing sector, and the economy relies mainly on subsistence agriculture. Tea and coffee are exported.

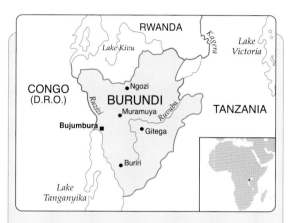

NATIONAL DATA – BURUNDI

Land area 25,650 sq km (9,904 sq mi)

Climate	Altitude m (ft)	Temperatures January °C(°F)	July °C(°F)	Annual precipitation mm (in)
Bujumbura	815 (2,674)	24 (75)	23 (73)	848 (33.3)

Major physical features largest lake: Lake Tanganyika (part) 32,900 sq km (12,700 sq mi)

Population (2006 est.) 8,090,068

Form of government republic

Armed forces army 45.000

Capital city Bujumbura (342,449)

Official languages Kirundi, French

Ethnic composition Hutu (Bantu) 85%; Tutsi (Hamitic) 14%; Twa (Pygmy) 1%; Europeans 3,000, South Asians 2,000

Religious affiliations Christian 67% (Roman Catholic 62%; Protestant 5%); traditional beliefs 23%; Muslim 10%

Currency 1 Burundi franc (BIF) = 100 centimes

Gross domestic product (2006 est.) U.S. $5.744 billion

Gross domestic product per capita (2006 est.) U.S. $700

Life expectancy at birth male 50.07 yr; female 51.58 yr

Major resources nickel, uranium, rare earth oxides, peat, cobalt, copper, platinum, vanadium, hydropower, niobium, tantalum, gold, tin, tungsten, kaolin, limestone, bananas, beans, cassava, coffee, coconuts, columbium, maize/corn, peat, phosphates, sweet potatoes, tea, timber

UGANDA

The East African Republic of Uganda is a landlocked state bordering the northeastern shores of huge Lake Victoria. Rich in natural resources such as copper and gold and with a once spectacular wildlife heritage, the country has been shamelessly ravaged by tyrannical rulers and torn apart by civil war in recent decades. Since 1986, however, it has slowly started to return to stability and economic prosperity.

NATIONAL DATA - UGANDA

Land area	199,710 sq km (77,108 sq mi)			

Climate		Temperatures		Annual
	Altitude m (ft)	January °C(°F)	July °C(°F)	precipitation mm (in)
Kampala	1,150 (3,773)	23 (67)	21 (70)	1,150 (46.2)

Major physical features highest point: Mount Stanley 5,109 m (16,763 ft); largest lake: Lake Victoria (part) 62,940 sq km (24,300 sq mi)

Population (2006 est.) 28,195,754

Form of government republic with one legislative house part-elected by popular vote

Armed forces joint forces 45,000

Largest cities Kampala (1,455,027)

Official languages English, Swahili

Ethnic composition Baganda 17%; Ankole 8%; Basoga 8%; Iteso 8%; Bakiga 7%; Langi 6%; Rwanda 6%; Bagisu 5%; Acholi 4%; Lugbara 4%; Batoro 3%; Bunyoro 3%; Alur 2%; Bagwere 2%; Bakonjo 2%; Jopodhola 2%; Karamojong 2%; Rundi 2%; non-African (European, Asian, Arab) 1%; other 8%

Religious affiliations Roman Catholic 33%; Protestant 33%; Muslim 16%; traditional beliefs 18%

Currency 1 Ugandan shilling (UGX) = 100 cents

Gross domestic product (2006 est.) U.S. $51.89 billion

Gross domestic product per capita (2006 est.) U.S. $1,800

Life expectancy at birth male 51.68 yr; female 53.69 yr

Major resources copper, cobalt, gold, hydropower, limestone, salt, coffee, cotton, tea, tobacco, bananas, fish, livestock, maize/corn, millet, phosphates, sorghum, sugarcane, timber, yams, tourism

Geography

Most of the land occupies a northward-sloping plateau north and west of Lake Victoria. In the far southwest the border with Rwanda runs through the volcanic Virunga Mountains. The western border with the Democratic Republic of the Congo runs parallel to the western branch of the Great Rift Valley, features of which include Lake Edward, the Ruwenzori Mountain Range (rising to the country's highest point, Mount Stanley), and Lake Albert. The Nile River flows north to Lake Victoria through Lake Kyoga, then north and west into Lake Albert, and finally north to Sudan.

The country has an equatorial climate, moderated by its altitude and also by large areas of lake and swampland. The north has a single wet season, whereas the south has two rainy seasons. Tropical forest grows around Lake Victoria, and wooded savanna parkland is found in the center and north. Uganda's varied wildlife, which includes lions, buffaloes, elephants, giraffes, hippos, and gorillas—as well as birds such as

Lake Bunyonyi lies in southwest Uganda. Supporting a variety of birdlife and other animals, it is the deepest crater lake in the country and a popular tourist attraction. Lakes and swamps cover one-sixth of Uganda's land area.

fish eagles, sacred ibises, and crowned cranes—is mostly protected within national parks and game reserves.

History

Once the site of several African kingdoms, the area known as Buganda rose to dominance in the 18th century. In 1894 it became a British protectorate, incorporating neighboring kingdoms in 1896. Independence was gained in 1963, with Mutesa II (1924–69), the king of Buganda, as first president. He was ousted by Milton Obote (1924–2005) in 1966, who declared the country a republic. Obote's rule was punctuated by corruption and human rights abuses, and he was deposed in a military coup by Idi Amin (c.1925–2003) while attending a commonwealth summit in Singapore. When Amin's disastrous regime ended (*see box right*), Obote became president for a second term, but this proved to be no more successful

THE RISE AND FALL OF IDI AMIN

Idi Amin was one of the world's most infamous despots. Born about 1925, he served in the King's African rifles when Uganda was a British colony. In 1971 he seized power in a coup and began a dictatorial reign of terror, ruthlessly suppressing political opponents, humiliating Europeans living in Uganda, and expelling Ugandan Asians—the driving force behind the economy. At the same time he espoused radical Arab extremism and was even suspected of cannibalism. In 1979 he was forced to flee Uganda after losing a war with Tanzania, and he died in exile in Saudi Arabia in 2003.

than the first. After coups in 1985 and 1986 Yoweri Museveni (b. 1944) took power, facing civil war, poor relations with Kenya, and the burden of some 100,000 refugees. However, the country appears to be returning to relative stability and economic growth once more.

Economy

During the 1990s the economy gradually stabilized, inflation fell, and there was significant investment in infrastructure and in projects designed to boost agricultural production and manufacturing. About 80 percent of the workforce is involved in agriculture, which benefits from fertile soils and regular rainfall. Coffee, tea, cotton, and tobacco are the principal exports. The country is also rich in minerals, including copper, cobalt, and gold. Power is chiefly in the form of hydroelectricity supplied by the Owen Falls Dam on the Nile River.

Uganda's dramatic scenery—such as at the Murchison Falls, where the Nile River plunges 122 m (400 ft) in three thunderous cascades—and its animal and plant life, are helping revive the tourist industry. Debt relief, coupled with the return of some of the exiled Ugandan Asian entrepreneurs, has also helped boost the economy. In addition to improving the road network, there is a plan to establish a direct rail link between Kampala and Johannesburg in South Africa.

Healthcare is poor and, as with many sub-Saharan countries, infection from HIV/AIDS and related death rates are very high.

KENYA

With its stunning scenery, spectacular wildlife, and golden beaches, Kenya was once a favorite tourist destination, as well as being the regional hub for East African trade and finance. Kenya was once regarded as a model of African stability. However, political violence, mismanagement and corruption, and a drought that has ravaged parts of the country have seriously dented this reputation and may damage the economy.

NATIONAL DATA – KENYA

Land area	569,250 sq km (219,789 sq mi)			

Climate		Temperatures		Annual
	Altitude m (ft)	January °C(°F)	July °C(°F)	precipitation mm (in)
Nairobi	1,616 (5,302)	18 (67)	15 (70)	1,024 (40.3)

Major physical features highest point: Mount Kenya 5,199 m (17,058 ft); longest river: Tana 708 km (440 mi)

Population (2006 est.) 34,707,817

Form of government multiparty republic with one legislative house

Armed forces army 20,000; navy 1,620; air force 2,500

Largest cities Nairobi (capital – 2,982,226); Mombasa (847,626); Nakuru (273,039); Eldoret (237,398)

Official languages Swahili, English

Ethnic composition Kikuyu 22%; Luhya 14%; Luo 13%; Kalenjin 12%; Kamba 11%; Kisii 6%; Meru 6%; other African 15%; non-African 1%

Religious affiliations Protestant 45%; Roman Catholic 33%; traditional beliefs 10%; Muslim 10%; other 2%

Currency 1 Kenyan shilling (KES) = 100 cents

Gross domestic product (2006 est.) U.S. $40.77 billion

Gross domestic product per capita (2006 est.) U.S. $1,200

Life expectancy at birth male 49.78 yr; female 48.07 yr

Major resources limestone, soda ash, salt, gemstones, fluorspar, zinc, diatomite, gypsum, wildlife, hydropower, tourism, bananas, beans, cattle, cassava, coffee, cotton, maize/corn, millet, potatoes, pyrethrum, sisal, sugarcane, sweet potatoes, tea

Geography

Straddling the equator, Kenya has a coastline on the Indian Ocean. The coastal plain is narrow in the south, but it broadens out northward toward the border with Somalia. Inland, the great Nyika Plain rises northward from the coast, and to the west lie the volcanic mountains of the Western Highlands. The mountains are split in two by the north–south course of the Great Rift Valley. Two large rivers, the Tana and the Galana, drain southeastward from the highlands across the Nyika Plain. To the west of the highlands, bordering Lake Victoria, there are grasslands. The southwest is the most fertile part of Kenya and also the most densely populated. By contrast, many other parts are arid and desertlike. Some of Kenya's wildlife is protected in

opposition failed to dislodge the KANU party and failed again in elections in 1997. Mwai Kibaki (b. 1931) of the multiethnic opposition group the National Rainbow Coalition defeated the KANU candidate in 2002 and became president, promising to curb corruption.

Economy

Primarily an agriculturally based economy for both subsistence and export earnings, the majority of the farming is based in the high-rainfall areas of the highlands, the central Rift Valley, and around Lake Victoria. Coffee and tea are the main cash crops, with staples consisting mainly of maize/corn, potatoes, pulses, millet, and bananas. The economy has been hampered in recent years by a reliance on goods whose prices have remained low, and by corruption. Tourism, once a valuable foreign exchange earner, has also suffered because of the fear of violence. A severe drought in 1998 to 2000 made problems worse. Loans from the IMF were halted in 2001 amid accusations that anticorruption measures were not being enforced. Erratic rainfall and corruption in 2002 continued to slow the economy. The government elected in 2003 began the task of halting corruption and encouraging investment and donor support. Despite its problems, Kenya has a good basic infrastructure.

reserves, such as the Tsavo and Nairobi National Parks. The climate is equatorial all year around.

History

Kenya became a British colony in 1920, but African nationalism in the 1950s led to a terror campaign by a Kikuyu anticolonial organization known as the Mau Mau. In 1964, a year after independence, Kenya was declared a republic, and Jomo Kenyatta (c.1889–1978), Kikuyu leader of the Kenya African National Union (KANU), became president. The country became a one-party state under Kenyatta and his successor Daniel arap Moi (b. 1924), but by 1991 violent demonstrations had led to the legalization of opposition parties, and in 1992 the country held its first multiparty elections. The

THE NOMADIC MASAI PEOPLE

The Masai—a group of tall East African nomadic people—once herded their cattle over the highlands of Kenya. However, in the early years of the 20th century the British relocated them to southern Kenya and Tanzania, where they now live. The Masai have for the most part shunned the trappings of westernism embraced by many other Kenyans, and prefer instead to live in clusters of cow-dung huts constructed by the women and to carry on their traditional pastoral lifestyle—a way of life now threatened by severe drought. Today the Masai number about 250,000.

TANZANIA

Tanzania was formed in 1964 by the union of mainland Tanganyika with Zanzibar, which consists of the Indian Ocean islands of Zanzibar and Pemba. Apart from the coastal plain, most of mainland Tanzania is a plateau traversed by mountains and depressions. Snowcapped Mount Kilimanjaro, Africa's highest peak, is in the north. Savanna and woodland cover much of the land, and there is alpine desert at higher altitudes. Some of the oldest-known human remains, dating back several million years, have been found in the Olduvai Gorge in the northeast of the country. For many years after independence the country had one-party rule, but in 1995 democratic elections were held. Today Tanzania is one of the least urbanized countries in Africa, with many different ethnic groups.

Tanzania is a poor country and relies heavily on agriculture, which accounts for nearly half of its GDP, much of its exports, and employs 80 percent of the workforce. Large swathes of the country are unsuitable for cattle or human habitation because of tsetse fly infestations, however, and the topography and climate also limit agriculture in many places; only 4 percent of the land is suitable for farming. Industries are mainly based around the processing of agricultural products and the manufacture of light consumer goods. Tanzania relies on international funding but is slowly improving its economy and infrastructure.

Much of Tanzania's wildlife is found within its game reserves. Among the best known are the Serengeti National Park and, below, the Ngorogoro Game Reserve—where thousands of flamingoes gather to feed and breed.

NATIONAL DATA - TANZANIA

Land area	886,037 sq km (342,101 sq mi)			

Climate	Altitude m (ft)	Temperatures January °C(°F)	July °C(°F)	Annual precipitation mm (in)
Salaam	58 (190)	27 (81)	23 (74)	1,056 (41.6)

Major physical features highest point: Kilimanjaro 5,895 m (19,341 ft); largest lake: Victoria (part) 62,940 sq km (24,300 sq mi)

Population (2006 est.) 37,445,392

Form of government multiparty republic with one legislative house

Armed forces army 23,000; navy 1,000; air force 3,000

Largest cities Dar es Salaam (2,915,878); Mwanza (480,279); Dodoma (capital - 196,006)

Official languages Swahili, English

Ethnic composition African 99% (of which 95% are Bantu consisting of more than 130 tribes); other 1%

Religious affiliations mainland - Christian 30%, Muslim 35%, traditional beliefs 35%; Zanzibar more than 99% Muslim

Currency 1 Tanzanian shilling (TZS) = 100 cents

Gross domestic product (2006 est.) U.S. $29.25 billion

Gross domestic product per capita (2006 est.) U.S. $800

Life expectancy at birth male 44.93 yr; female 46.37 yr

Major resources hydropower, tin, phosphates, iron ore, coal, diamonds, gemstones, gold, natural gas, nickel, beans, cassava, cloves, coconuts, coffee, cotton, maize/corn, sisal, tobacco

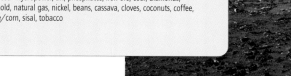

MOZAMBIQUE

Mozambique is situated on Africa's southeastern coast, with its east coast facing Madagascar across the Mozambique Channel. A wide coastal plain occupies most of the south, but it becomes narrower to the north. Inland the terrain rises to form the tablelands of the High Veld. In the northwest the land drops down to the shores of Lake Malawi. The main vegetation is savanna, woodland, and grassland, with mangroves and palms along the coast. Wildlife is still reasonably abundant.

Following independence in 1975 the country began to suffer from economic mismanagement, mass white emigration, drought, civil war, and a dependence on South Africa. At that time Mozambique was perhaps the world's poorest country. However, the ruling Front for the Liberation of Mozambique abandoned Marxism in 1989, and a new constitution encouraged multiparty elections. Since then free market reforms have helped stabilize the economy, and foreign aid has also been forthcoming. Nevertheless, most of the population lives below the poverty line, and subsistence agriculture, with maize/corn as the chief staple, employs the majority of the workforce. The presence of tsetse flies limits livestock rearing in many areas. New industries such as smelting, precious metal extraction, and garment manufacturing are developing, however, and they should help improve the country's economic outlook.

Mozambique's economy is largely based around agriculture, and about 80 percent of the workforce is engaged in farming, often living in small rural communities like the one shown here.

NATIONAL DATA – MOZAMBIQUE

Land area	784,090 sq km (302,739 sq mi)			

Climate		Temperatures		Annual
	Altitude m (ft)	January °C(°F)	July °C(°F)	precipitation mm (in)
Maputo	60 (197)	27 (80)	19 (56)	814 (32)

Major physical features highest point: Monte Binga 2,436 m (7,992 ft)

Population (2006 est.) 19,686,505

Form of government multiparty republic with one legislative house

Armed forces army 10,000; navy 200; air force 1,000

Largest cities Maputo (capital – 1,249,309); Matola (570,242); Beira (561,151); Nampula (407,338)

Official language Portuguese

Ethnic composition Traditional tribal groups 99.66% (Makhuwa, Tsonga, Lomwe, Sena, and others); Europeans 0.06%; Euro-Africans 0.2%; Indians 0.08%

Religious affiliations Catholic 23.8%; Muslim 17.8%; Zionist Christian 17.5%; other 17.8%; none 23.1%

Currency 1 metical (MZM) = 100 centavos

Gross domestic product (2006 est.) U.S. $29.32 billion

Gross domestic product per capita (2006 est.) U.S. $1,500

Life expectancy at birth male 39.53 yr; female 40.13 yr

Major resources coal, titanium, natural gas, hydropower, tantalum, graphite, clothing, bananas, cashew nuts, cassava, cereals, coconuts, sisal, tea

ZAMBIA

NATIONAL DATA – ZAMBIA

Land area	740,724 sq km (285,995 sq mi)			

Climate		Temperatures		Annual
	Altitude m (ft)	January °C(°F)	July °C(°F)	precipitation mm (in)
Lusaka	1,297 (4,195)	22 (71	16 (61)	843 (33.1)

Major physical features highest point: Nyika Plateau (part) 2,164 m (7,100 ft)

Population (2006 est.) 11,502,010

Form of government multiparty republic with one legislative house

Armed forces army 13,500; navy 1,600; air force 1,400

Capital city Lusaka (1,346,522)

Official language English

Ethnic composition Bemba 36.2%; Maravi 17.6%; Tonga 15.1%; Northwestern tribes 10.1%; Barotze 8.2%; Mambwe 4.6%; Tumbuka 4.6%; others 3.6%

Religious affiliations Christian 50%–75%, Muslim and Hindu 24%–49%, indigenous beliefs 1%

Currency 1 Zambian kwacha (ZMK) = 100 ngwee

Gross domestic product (2006 est.) U.S. $11.51 billion

Gross domestic product per capita (2006 est.) U.S. $1,000

Life expectancy at birth male 39.76 yr; female 40.31 yr

Major resources copper, cobalt, zinc, lead, coal, emeralds, gold, silver, uranium, hydropower, fisheries, cassava, cattle, groundnuts, maize/corn, tobacco, sugarcane

Water from the Zambezi River's Victoria Falls on the Zambia/Zimbabwe border plunges 108 m (354 ft), creating mist clouds that soar up to 500 m (1,600 ft) above the chasm.

Zambia's landscape is mostly high, rolling plateau broken by mountains and deep valleys, and most of the country is covered with savanna and woodland, with forests in the southwest, consisting chiefly of valuable Rhodesian teak. The country's subtropical climate is moderated by its elevation and location.

The territory of Northern Rhodesia became Zambia upon independence in 1964. The elections in 1991 ended one-party rule, but subsequent elections have been tainted by the harassment of opposition parties and challenges to the validity of elected candidates. Opposition parties currently hold a majority of seats in the National Assembly. Agriculture employs almost 85 percent of the workforce, and most export crops are grown on large European-run farms. Copper was once the mainstay of the economy but now accounts for under 55 percent of exports. Although Zambia has attempted to improve its economy, living standards have fallen and extreme poverty is still rife.

MALAWI

Situated at the southern end of the Great Rift Valley, Malawi's dominant feature is the elongate Lake Malawi, which occupies about one-fifth of the country's total area. The Shire River runs south through a deep swampy valley. Central and western Malawi consist mostly of plateaus, with high mountains in the north. Much of the original woodland has been cleared for cultivation, and large animals are mainly confined to reserves, although hippos are found in Lake Malawi.

Malawi was formerly the British protectorate of Nyasaland. Malawi achieved independence in 1964, soon becoming a single-party republic until multiparty elections were held for the first time in 1994. However, corruption, pressure on agricultural land, and disease pose major problems for the country. Malawi is one of the world's poorest and least developed countries and depends on foreign aid from various quarters. Literacy is low and housing is in short supply. The country also has a growing HIV/AIDS epidemic and experiences one of the highest death rates in the world.

Nearly 90 percent of the population lives in rural areas and is engaged in farming. Maize/corn is the chief staple, and cash crops include tobacco, sugarcane, and tea. The economy is overreliant on tobacco, however, which accounts for two-thirds of exports. Fishing, mostly from Lake Malawi, is also an important industry. Mineral resources are few, but there is abundant water and hydroelectric potential. The road system is limited, and most roads are unsurfaced.

Cattle resting by a river in Malawi. The country has a highly rural economy, with over 85 percent of the workforce engaged in subsistence agriculture.

NATIONAL DATA – MALAWI

Land area	94,080 sq km (36,324 sq mi)			

Climate		Temperatures		Annual
	Altitude m (ft)	January °C(°F)	July °C(°F)	precipitation mm (in)
Lilongwe	1,095 (3,593)	22 (71)	15 (59)	775 (30.5)

Major physical features highest point: Mount Mulanje 3,000 m (9,843 ft); longest river: Shire (part) 400 km (250 mi); largest lake: Lake Malawi 29,600 sq km (11,400 sq mi)

Population (2006 est.) 13,013,926

Form of government multiparty republic with one legislative house

Armed forces army 5,300

Largest cities Blantyre (618,153); Lilongwe (capital – 721,988); Mzuzu (143,320); Zomba (86.217)

Official language English

Ethnic composition Maravi 58.3%; Lomwe 18.4%; Yao 13.2%; Ngoni 6.7%; others 3.4%

Religious affiliations Christian 79.9%; Muslim 12.8%; other 3%; none 4.3%

Currency 1 Malawian kwacha (MWK) = 100 tambala

Gross domestic product (2006 est.) U.S. $8.038 billion

Gross domestic product per capita (2006 est.) U.S. $600

Life expectancy at birth male 41.93 yr; female 41.45 yr

Major resources limestone (marble), hydropower, unexploited uranium, coal and bauxite, beans, cassava, cotton, groundnuts, maize/corn, millet, sugarcane, sorghum, tobacco, tea

SEYCHELLES

The Seychelles is an archipelago of about 100 islands in the Indian Ocean north of Madagascar. The 40 or so islands in the man group, including the largest island, Mahé, are granitic and consist of a mountainous heart surrounded by a flat coastal strip. The mostly smaller outer islands are made from coral accretions and form reefs and atolls. They are almost flat or only slightly elevated. Most of these islands have no fresh water, and few are inhabited. The main islands have high humidity and rainfall, supporting the remnants of the lush tropical rain forest that once covered them.

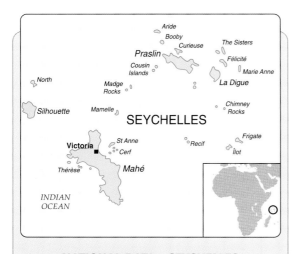

The beautiful, palm-fringed coral beaches of the Seychelles have played a major part in the economy of the islands, attracting many tourists and employing about 30 percent of the workforce.

The Seychelles occupy a strategic sea route on the way from Europe to India. France annexed the islands in 1756, but they passed to Britain after the Napoleonic Wars. The islands gained independence in 1976. Albert René (b. 1935) seized power in a coup in 1979, but he was reelected in the first multiparty elections in 1993. He stepped down in 2004, and Vice President James Michel (b. 1944) became president.

Since independence the economy of the Seychelles has grown steadily. The chief industries are tourism, which brings in about 70 percent of hard currency earnings, and tuna fishing. Foreign investment has been used to upgrade hotels and other services, but the government has also tried to reduce the dependence on tourism by promoting farming, fishing, and manufacturing. Copra, tobacco, cinnamon, vanilla, and coconuts are exported, but much food is imported. Industry is largely in the form of food processing.

NATIONAL DATA – SEYCHELLES

Land area 455 sq km (176 sq mi)

Climate	Altitude m (ft)	Temperatures January °C(°F)	July °C(°F)	Annual precipitation mm (in)
Victoria	3 (10)	27 (80)	26 (56)	2,172 (85.5)

Major physical features largest island: Mahé 153 sq km (59 sq mi)

Population (2006 est.) 81,541

Form of government multiparty republic with one legislative house

Armed forces army 200

Capital city Victoria (22,336)

Official languages English, French, Creole

Ethnic composition Seychellois Creole (Asian/African/European) 89.1%; Indian 4.7%; Malagasy 3.1%; Chinese 1.6%; English 1.5%

Religious affiliations Roman Catholic 82.3%, Anglican 6.4%, Seventh Day Adventist 1.1%, other Christian 3.4%, Hindu 2.1%, Muslim 1.1%, other non-Christian 1.5%, unspecified 1.5%, none 0.6%

Currency 1 Seychelles rupee (SCR) = 100 cents

Gross domestic product (2002 est.) U.S. $626 million

Gross domestic product per capita (2002 est.) U.S. $7,800

Life expectancy at birth male 66.69 yr; female 77.63 yr

Major resources fish, coconuts, copra, cinnamon, tobacco, vanilla, tourism, fruit

COMOROS

Comoros is a group of volcanic islands in the Indian Ocean—Mayotte is still a French dependency. Inland the islands' terrain varies from steep mountains to low hills clad with forests. Comoros has experienced 19 coups or attempted coups since independence in 1975, but the political situation is now more stable, with each island enjoying a degree of autonomy within a federalist union. Comoros is a poor nation with few natural resources. Most workers are engaged in subsistence agriculture. Foreign aid and money sent home by Comorans working overseas are vital to the economy.

NATIONAL DATA - COMOROS

Land area	2,170 sq km (837 sq mi)			
Climate		Temperatures		Annual precipitation
	Altitude m (ft)	January °C(°F)	July °C(°F)	mm (in)
Moroni	12 (39)	27 (81)	23 (73)	2,542 (100)

Major physical features highest point: Mount Karthala (Njazidja) 2,361 m (7,746 ft); largest island: Njazidja 1,148 sq km (443 sq mi)
Population (2006 est.) 690,948
Form of government federal multiparty republic with one legislative house
Armed forces army 700 (reorganized in 1995); navy 200
Capital city Moroni (44,518)
Official languages Arabic, French
Ethnic composition Comorian (Bantu/Arab/Malagasy) 96.9%; Makua 1.6%; French 0.4%; others 1.1%
Official religion Islam
Religious affiliations Sunni Muslim 98%; Roman Catholic 2%
Currency 1 Comoran franc (KMF) = 100 centimes
Gross domestic product (2002) U.S. $441 million
Gross domestic product per capita (2005) U.S. $600
Life expectancy at birth male 60 yr; female 64.72 yr
Major resources negligible apart from cash crops such as vanilla, copra, cloves, ylang-ylang, coffee, sweet potatoes, rice, coconut, maize/corn, yams

MAURITIUS

One of the Mascarene islands, Mauritius lies about 800 km (500 mi) east of Madagascar. Its territory also includes the volcanic island of Rodrigues and the tiny dependency of Agalegals. Mauritius's coral reef-fringed coastal plain rises to the remains of a huge volcano. Much of the island's forest has been cleared. A stable democracy, Mauritius has attracted much foreign investment (about 10,000 foreign companies—mainly Indian and South African—have bases here), and the republic has moved from a low-income farming economy to a middle-income diversified economy based on industrial, financial, and tourist sectors.

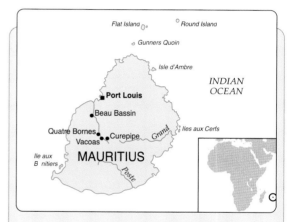

NATIONAL DATA - MAURITIUS

Land area	2,030 sq km (784 sq mi)			
Climate		Temperatures		Annual precipitation
	Altitude m (ft)	January °C(°F)	July °C(°F)	mm (in)
Port Louis	55 (180)	28 (72)	23 (59)	711 (27.9)

Major physical features highest point: Piton de la Petite Rivière Noire 826 m (2,711 ft); largest island: Mauritius 1,865 sq km (720 sq mi)
Population (2006 est.) 1,240,827
Form of government multiparty republic with one legislative house
Armed forces Paramilitary 2,000
Capital city Port Louis (158,196)
Official language English
Ethnic composition Indo-Mauritian 68%; Creole 27%; Sino-Mauritian 3%; Franco-Mauritian 2%
Religious affiliations Hindu 48%; Roman Catholic 23.6%; other Christian 8.6%; Muslim 16.6%, other 2.5%; unspecified 0.3%; none 0.4%
Currency 1 Mauritian rupee (MUR) = 100 cents
Gross domestic product (2006 est.) U.S. $16.72 billion
Gross domestic product per capita (2006 est.) U.S. $13,500
Life expectancy at birth male 68.66 yr; female 76.66 yr
Major resources sugarcane, tea, bananas, fish, tourism, potatoes, tobacco

The state of Madagascar is the fourth largest island in the world. Geologically, it was formed when it broke away from the landmass of Africa about 50 million years ago. It remains very different from the African mainland, not least in its people and their culture, and in its unique and diverse wildlife—much of it now under threat. The island maintains strong links with France as well as with former French colonies in West Africa.

NATIONAL DATA – MADAGASCAR

Land area	581,540 sq km (224,534 sq mi)			
Climate		Temperatures		Annual
	Altitude m (ft)	January °C(°F)	July °C(°F)	precipitation mm (in)
Antananarivo	1,310 (4,297)	22 (72)	15 (59)	1,365 (25.9)

Major physical features highest point: Tsaratanana Massif 2,876 m (9,436 ft); longest river: Mangoky 560 km (350 mi)
Population (2006 est.) 18,595,469
Form of government multiparty republic with one legislative house
Armed forces army 12,500; navy 500; air force 500
Capital city Antananarivo (1,538,349)
Official languages French, Malagasy
Ethnic composition Malagasy 98.9%; Comorian 0.3%; Indian 0.2%; French 0.2%; others 0.4%
Religious affiliations traditional beliefs 52%; Christian 41%; Muslim 7%
Currency 1 Madagascar ariary (MGA) = 5 iraimbilanja
Gross domestic product (2006 est.) U.S. $17.27 billion
Gross domestic product per capita (2006 est.) U.S. $900
Life expectancy at birth male 54.93 yr; female 59.82 yr
Major resources graphite, chromite, gold, coal, bauxite, salt, quartz, tar sands, precious stones, mica, fish, hydropower, tourism, bananas, cassava, cloves, coffee, maize/corn, peppers, potatoes, rice, sisal, sugarcane, vanilla, zirconia

Geography

The east coast is lined with coral beaches and lagoons, and from here the land rises steeply to the great central plateau that covers most of the island. This is ridged and crossed by many rivers and is interspersed by mountain massifs. The highest is the Massif du Tsaratanana in the north. There are volcanic features such as crater lakes and steep sea cliffs in the far north and south. On the western side the mountains fall away more gradually, and here rivers such as the Ikopa and the Mangoky meander through gentler landscapes, washing rich sediments to the broad coastal plains.

The climate is very varied, ranging from temperate in the highlands to tropical along the coasts. Heavy seasonal rains occur in the north and east, but conditions are relatively dry in the central highlands and semiarid in the south. Until recently most of the island was clad in forests, ranging from tropical rain forest to cooler evergreen and deciduous woodlands.

However, a slash-and-burn cultivation policy has devastated the forests, and only small areas are left. The exposed soil is now suffering from severe erosion.

Society

Madagascar was probably first settled before the 10th century by Indonesian seafarers. In about the 14th century African mainland settlers were joined by Arab and Asian traders, who brought Muslim influences. In the 16th century a French trading post was established, and about this time the Malagasy people settled the interior, establishing powerful kingdoms. Over the next 100 years or more the rulers of these kingdoms were courted by both the French and the British, but the island became a French overseas territory after World War II. It gained independence in 1960. In 1975 the island broke ties with France and sought to align itself with the Soviet bloc. In 1976, following a series of coups, Commander Didier Ratsiraka (b. 1936) became president. Free presidential elections were held in 1992–93, following the approval of a new constitution.

Species of baobabs, Adansonia, *are widespread in the south and west of Madagascar. Like their relatives on mainland Africa, they have massive trunks.*

MADAGASCAN WILDLIFE

Madagascar's isolation has allowed a unique and rich diversity of wildlife to evolve. This includes the small, spiny, insectivorous tenrec and many species of lemurs (primitive primates). There are also crocodiles, chameleons, butterflies, and many birds. Sea fish native to the area include the spiny globefish and a famous "living fossil" called the coelacanth. The wildlife has been devastated, however, by deliberate killing and by habitat destruction. Several lemur species have become extinct, and those remaining are in danger. Conservation efforts are small scale and probably too late.

Economy

The economy of Madagascar suffered as a result of the abrupt transition to state planning that followed the 1975 revolution. However, Madagascar discarded socialist economics in the mid-1990s and adopted a free-market strategy that has helped the country slowly improve its wealth. Nevertheless, the World Bank estimates that 70 percent of the population lives on less than $1 per day. Only a few roads are surfaced, but rail and port facilities are good, as are internal and international air services.

The country still relies heavily on traditional agriculture. The majority of its exports are of cash crops such as coffee, cloves, vanilla, sisal, and sugar; they amount to more than one-quarter of GDP. Cattle are the main livestock and are largely reared for local consumption. The main staple crops are cassava and rice, but the island is not self-sufficient in either, and production cannot keep pace with the fast-growing population. Fishing has not been fully developed and remains more or less a subsistence occupation. Chromite and graphite are mined for export, together with small amounts of gold and precious stones. There are no energy resources except for hydroelectricity, which fulfils half the country's needs; the rest is imported. Manufacturing industry is based largely on agriculture, and typical products include soap, textiles, sisal rope, sugar, and other processed foods. There is a printing works and a vehicle-assembly plant in the capital.

ANGOLA

The large state of Angola also includes the enclave of Cabinda. Inland from the cooler, narrow coastal plains the land rises to an extensive tableland covering 60 percent of the country. From the central highlands a network of rivers fans out; some flow to the Atlantic, while others feed the rivers of adjoining countries. The climate is generally hot. Vegetation varies from tropical rain forest in Cabinda and the north to savanna wood and grassland in the south, with some coastal desert.

NATIONAL DATA – ANGOLA

Land area	1,246,700 sq km (481,354 sq mi)

Climate	Altitude m (ft)	Temperatures January °C(°F)	July °C(°F)	Annual precipitation mm (in)
Luanda	44 (144)	26 (67)	21 (70)	323 (12.7)

Major physical features	highest point: Mount Moco 2,559 m (8,397 ft)
Population	(2006 est.) 12,127,071
Form of government	presidential multiparty republic
Armed forces	army 100,000; navy 1,000; air force 6,000
Capital city	Luanda (2,977,212)
Official language	Portuguese
Ethnic composition	Ovimbundu 37%; Kimbundu 25%; Bakongo 13%; Mestico (mixed European and native African) 2%; European 1%; other 22%
Religious affiliations	traditional beliefs 47%; Roman Catholic 38%; Protestant 15%
Currency	1 kwanza (AOA) = 100 centimos
Gross domestic product	(2006 est.) U.S. $51.95 billion
Gross domestic product per capita	(2006 est.) U.S. $4,300
Life expectancy at birth	male 37.47 yr; female 39.83 yr
Major resources	petroleum, natural gas, diamonds, iron ore, phosphates, copper, feldspar, gold, bauxite, uranium, asphalt, bananas, cassava, citrus fruits, coffee, cotton, fish, maize/corn, palm oil, salt, sisal, sugar beet, sweet potatoes, timber

Angolan village life. The long civil war caused deforestation, displacement, and the loss of land through the laying of land mines, and seriously disrupted the lives of the peasant farmers.

The year 2002 saw the end of a 27-year civil war that may have accounted for 1.5 million lives and the displacement of a further 4 million people. During the civil war Angola's economy was in disarray, but now it is slowly improving. Subsistence agriculture provides a livelihood for many, but most food is imported. The country has rich reserves of timber, and coastal fishing brings in sardines and mackerel. However, it is the extensive petroleum and natural gas fields that are the main source of foreign income. Oil production and associated activities account for more than half of the country's exports, although diamonds are also an important export commodity. Apart from petroleum, the main manufacturing industry is steel processing. Other, smaller, industries mainly serve the home market.

BOTSWANA

Landlocked Botswana forms part of the southern African plateau. The landscape is mainly flat to gently rolling tableland, with the dry scrubby Kalahari Desert in the west and savanna grassland in the east. In the north and east are the river basins of the Okavango, the Chobe, and the Limpopo, where most of the country's surface water is situated. The climate varies from semiarid to subtropical. Rainfall is scanty and unpredictable, and droughts can last for years.

Since independence in 1966, Botswana has enjoyed four decades of civilian government, progressive social policies, and significant capital investment to create one of Africa's most dynamic economies. Mining, principally for diamonds, is the key economic activity—accounting for over one-third of GDP and nearly 80 percent of export earnings—although conservation programs and extensive nature reserves have helped boost tourism. Financial services, subsistence farming, and cattle raising are also important industries. However, the country is still faced with poverty and high unemployment (possibly as much as 40 percent). Botswana's HIV/AIDS infection rates are the world's second highest, although it also has one of Africa's best programs for dealing with the disease.

Impala roaming on the savanna in Botswana. This type of grassland is the dominant vegetation in the country.

NATIONAL DATA – BOTSWANA

Land area	585,370 sq km (226,013 sq mi)			

Climate	Altitude m (ft)	Temperatures January °C(°F)	July °C(°F)	Annual precipitation mm (in)
Francistown	983 (3,225)	25 (77)	15 (59)	448 (17.6)

Major physical features highest point: Tsodilo Hills 1,375 m (4,511 ft)

Population (2006 est.) 1,639,833

Form of government multiparty republic with one legislative house

Armed forces army 8,500; air force 500

Capital city Gaborone (220,558)

Official language English

Ethnic composition Tswana (or Setswana) 79%; Kalanga 11%; Basarwa 3%; other, including Bushmen, Kgalagadi, and White 7%

Religious affiliations Christian 71.6%; Badimo 6%; other 1.4%; unspecified 0.4%; none 20.6%

Currency 1 pula (BWP) = 100 thebe

Gross domestic product (2006 est.) U.S. $18.72 billion

Gross domestic product per capita (2006 est.) U.S. $11,400

Life expectancy at birth male 33.9 yr; female 33.56 yr

Major resources diamonds, copper, nickel, salt, soda ash, potash, coal, iron ore, silver, asbestos, beans, cattle, meat processing, sorghum, manganese, maize/corn, tourism

ZIMBABWE

Formerly known as Southern Rhodesia, Zimbabwe is a landlocked state in the southeastern part of Africa bordered by Zambia, Botswana, South Africa, and Mozambique. The name Zimbabwe (meaning "houses of stone" in the Shona language) was taken from Great Zimbabwe—massive fortifications in the south of the country. Since 1980 the nation's once prosperous economy and infrastructure have been systematically devastated, and are a cause for international concern.

NATIONAL DATA – ZIMBABWE

Land area	386,670 sq km (149,294 sq mi)			
Climate		Temperatures		Annual precipitation
	Altitude m (ft)	January °C(°F)	July °C(°F)	mm (in)
Harare	1,479 (4,852)	21 (70)	14 (57)	841 (33.1)

Major physical features	highest point: Inyangani 2,592 m (8,504 ft)
Population	(2006 est.) 12,236,805
Form of government	one-party republic with one legislative house
Armed forces	army 25,000; navy 4,000; air force 21,800
Largest cities	Harare (capital – 1,607,022); Bulawayo (713,340); Chitungwiza (352,204); Mutare (193,629); Gweru (148,935)
Official language	English
Ethnic composition	Shona 82%; Ndebele 14%; other Africans 2.0%; Asian 1.0%;
Religious affiliations	syncretic (Christianity and indigenous beliefs) 50%; Christian 25%; indigenous 24%; others 1%
Currency	1 Zimbabwean dollar (ZWD) = 100 cents
Gross domestic product	(2006 est.) U.S. $25.05 billion
Gross domestic product per capita	(2006 est.) U.S. $2,000
Life expectancy at birth	male 40.39 yr; female 38.16 yr
Major resources	coal, chromium ore, asbestos, gold, nickel, iron ore, vanadium, lithium, tin, copper, platinum group metals, maize/corn, millet, sugarcane, wheat, tobacco

Geography

Zimbabwe is dominated by a broad mountainous ridge known as the High Veld, which spans the country from the southwest to the northeast. Southeast of Harare is Inyangani, the highest part of the escarpment that borders Mozambique. The mountains are flanked north and south by the Middle Veld. These fall away to the Low Veld of two great river basins. The Zambezi River on the northern border with Zambia plunges dramatically over the Victoria Falls in a series of gorges. Farther downstream the valley has been dammed and flooded to form Lake Kariba. The Limpopo River in the far south on the border with South Africa flows through much gentler country. Both rivers eventually flow out into the Indian Ocean via Mozambique.

Zimbabwe lies within the tropics, but its climate is modified by altitude and aspect. Winters are dry and cool, and rain is confined largely to the hot summer months. Rainfall is heaviest in the eastern mountains, which have evergreen forests. Land to the south, around the Limpopo, is arid in places. Most of the country's natural vegetation is savanna grassland and woodlands, but large areas have been felled for cultivation. The habitat of wildlife such as aardvarks, baboons, elephants, gorillas, hippos, and crocodiles is restricted, but some conservation measures have been adopted.

Society

The original inhabitants of the area were driven out by Bantu invaders, who built parts of Great Zimbabwe in the 9th century. Other Bantus arrived in the mid-19th century, along with Europeans. The British South Africa Company began to settle the country in the 1890s, in the face of uprisings from ethnic groups. In 1963 the federation with Northern Rhodesia and Nyasaland collapsed, and the European-dominated Rhodesian Front Party, led by Ian Smith (b. 1919), pressed for independence from Britain. Britain refused, and the Front made a unilateral declaration of independence (UDI) in 1965. UN sanctions and a guerrilla war waged by black opponents to the Smith government ensued, which led to free elections in 1979 and independence (as Zimbabwe) in 1980. Robert Mugabe (b. 1924) was elected prime minister and has ruled ever since.

Part of the Great Enclosure at Great Zimbabwe, the largest single ancient structure south of the Sahara. Great Zimbabwe was built by African people between 1250 and 1450 A.D.

Economy

The country's economy suffered during the bitter civil war and sanctions of the 1970s, although some sectors benefited from the lack of outside competition. For example, agriculture became more diversified. The larger farms, many of which were European-owned until Mugabe's land confiscation policy, produced most of the cash crops, including tobacco, cotton, and sugarcane, and employed a large proportion of the working population. Now many European farmers have left the country or been forced to quit their farms, and the new recipients of the land lack the skills to manage it successfully. The result of this policy is that most land is left uncultivated, hundreds of thousands are out of work, and there is a chronic shortage of basic food commodities. The tobacco crop, once a mainstay of the economy, is a fraction of its previous total, and exports are minimal. Drought has exacerbated the situation still further. Zimbabwe's 1998–2002 involvement in the war in the Democratic Republic of the Congo drained hundreds of millions of dollars from the economy.

Manufacturing was encouraged by sanctions pressure and became a much more significant part of the economy. Industries include mining, textiles, light machinery, and manufactured goods. Fuel is needed for electricity generation, but Zimbabwe cannot afford it.

The state of Namibia lies on the southwest coast of the African mainland. From its northeastern corner the narrow, fingerlike Caprivi Strip extends its territory eastward as far as Zambia. Namibia gained independence fairly recently from South Africa, in 1990, although the main port, Walvis Bay, was ceded only in 1994. The Namibian economy is still closely linked to that of South Africa.

NATIONAL DATA – NAMIBIA

Land area	825,418 sq km (318,696 sq mi)			
Climate		Temperatures		Annual
	Altitude m (ft)	January °C(°F)	July °C(°F)	precipitation mm (in)
Windhoek	1,738 (5,669	12 (54)	13 (56)	362 (14.2)

Major physical features	highest point: Mount Brand 2,574 m (8,445 ft)

Population	(2006 est.) 2,044,147

Form of government	multiparty republic with two legislative houses

Armed forces	army 9,000; navy 200

Capital city	Windhoek (286,762)

Official language	English

Ethnic composition	Ovambo 49.8%; Kavango 9.3%; Herero 7.5%; Damara 7.5%; European 6.4%; Nama (Hottentots) 4.8%; others 14.7%

Religious affiliations	Christian 80%-90% (Lutheran 50% at least); traditional beliefs 10%-20%

Currency	1 Namibian dollar (NAD) = 100 cents and 1 South African rand (ZAR) = 100 cents

Gross domestic product	(2006 est.) U.S. $15.04 billion

Gross domestic product per capita	(2006 est.) U.S. $7,400

Life expectancy at birth	male 44.46 yr; female 42.29 yr

Major resources	diamonds, copper, uranium, gold, silver, lead, tin, tungsten, lithium, cadmium, zinc, salt, hydropower, fish, possible deposits of oil, coal, and iron ore, cattle, maize/corn, millet, sorghum

Geography

The sand dunes of the Namib Desert extend from the coast toward the foot of the Great Escarpment that rims the great central plateau. The mountains of the escarpment are highest in the central portion around Windhoek. The plateau itself occupies the eastern part of the country and is covered by the dry scrub of the Kalahari Desert.

The Namib Desert supports little vegetation apart from succulents and the unusual welwitschia plant that absorbs moisture from sea fogs. The welwitschia plant—often described as a living fossil—can survive to a great age, with some specimens thought to be up to 2,000 years old. The desert also supports many specialized animal species, such as the Wedge-snouted Sand Lizard, the Barking Gecko, and the Namaqua Dune Molerat. Inland areas are less barren, with many drought-resistant grasses and shrubs, and savanna woodland in the far north. The wildlife here is typical of southern Africa: baboons, kudu antelopes, elephants, giraffes,

The Namib Desert, some 80,900 sq km (31,200 sq mi) in area, extends along the coast of western Namibia from the Uniab River in the north to the town of Luderitz in the south, and inland from the Atlantic coastline to the foot of the Namib Escarpment.

zebras, lions, and birds such as flamingoes. The climate of Namibia is generally hot and very dry. Seasonal rainfall is confined mainly to the north.

Society

Southwest Africa, as Namibia was formerly known, became a German protectorate in 1884. During World War I it was occupied by South Africa, to which it was mandated in 1920 by the League of Nations as a trust territory. In 1946 it came under the United Nations trusteeship system, despite South Africa's stated intention to annex the country. In 1966 the UN called for total South African withdrawal, and the Marxist South West Africa People's Organization (SWAPO) began a long guerrilla war against ongoing South African occupation. Free elections in 1989 brought SWAPO to power, and independence followed in 1990. Namibia is still economically dependent on South Africa, with which it remains in custom union, but it is gradually becoming more independent.

Economy

Most Namibians (nearly 50 percent of the workforce) work on the land, engaged in subsistence farming. However, the soils and climate do not favor agriculture. There is also a small-scale offshore fishing industry. This was once prosperous, but it was damaged by overfishing in the 1970s. It is now recovering. About half of Namibia's food is imported, mainly from South Africa (normally 50 percent of its annual cereal requirements come from abroad). In drought years food shortages are a major problem in rural areas. Namibia also depends on South Africa for much of its fuel and manufactured goods.

The country is rich in minerals, and the economy relies heavily on the extraction and reprocessing of minerals for export. Rich alluvial diamond deposits make the country a primary source of gem-quality diamonds. The country is also the fourth largest exporter of nonfuel minerals in Africa, the world's fifth largest producer of uranium, and it produces large quantities of copper, lead, zinc, tin, silver, and tungsten. Mining accounts for 20 percent of GDP, although it only employs a tiny proportion of the population. A high per capita GDP hides one of the world's most unequal distributions of income.

The transportation infrastructure is poor but improving, with most road and rail networks confined to the south. Healthcare is concentrated around a few large hospitals. Literacy is low outside the white community.

SOUTH AFRICA

A large country occupying the strategic southern tip of Africa, South Africa also encloses totally the small state of Lesotho. From 1948 South Africa's politics was dominated by the policy of apartheid, which involved the almost complete segregation of the white minority from the rest of the population. The policy began to be dismantled in 1991 following international sanctions and a guerrilla war waged against the government.

NATIONAL DATA – SOUTH AFRICA

Land area	1,219,912 sq km (471,011 sq mi)			

Climate	Altitude m (ft)	Temperatures January °C(°F)	July °C(°F)	Annual precipitation mm (in)
Cape Town	12 (39)	21 (70)	12 (59)	515 (20.2)

Population (2006 est.) 44,187,637

Form of government multiparty republic with two legislative houses

Armed forces army 36,000; navy 4.500; air force 9,250

Capital cities Cape Town (legislative - 3,660,197); Pretoria (administrative - 1,757,505); Bloemfontein (judicial - 498,404)

Official languages Afrikaans, Ndebele, Northern Sotho, Southern Sotho, Swati, Tsonga, Tswana, Venda, Xhosa, Zulu, English

Ethnic composition Black African 79%; White 9.6%; Mixed race 8.9%; Indian/Asian 2.5%

Religious affiliations Zion Christian 11.1%; Pentecostal/Charismatic 8.2%; Catholic 7.1%; Methodist 6.8%; Dutch Reformed 6.7%; Anglican 3.8%; other Christian 36%; Islam 1.5%; other 2.3%; unspecified 1.4%; none 15.1%

Currency 1 South African rand (ZAR) = 100 cents

Gross domestic product (2006 est) U.S. $576.4 billion

Gross domestic product per capita (2006 est.) U.S. $13,000

Life expectancy at birth male 43.25 yr; female 42.19 yr

Major resources gold, chromium, antimony, coal, iron ore, manganese, nickel, phosphates, tin, uranium, gem diamonds, platinum, copper, vanadium, salt, natural gas, fruits, maize/corn, cotton, potatoes, tobacco, livestock, tourism

Geography

The country has two main topographic areas: the vast saucer-shaped central plateau, and the lands that surround it. They are separated by the Great Escarpment, forming a rim around the central plateau from the Transvaal Drakensberg in the northeast to Namibia in the northwest. The central plateau, largely drained by the Orange (or Gariep) River, varies in altitude. Around the central plateau the land drops to the sea via a coastal plain that is generally narrow. Most of the country is in the warm temperate zone, and the climate is predominantly dry—half the country is arid or semiarid. Higher rainfall in the east creates savanna grassland. The west has semiarid scrub, and in the north there is bushland. The sandy Namib Desert runs along the west coast, but in the far southwest the vegetation is more Mediterranean. The varied wildlife—including

Outeniqua Pass in the Outeniqua Mountain range, situated in the Southern Cape area, is a popular tourist destination.

on the policy by the 1990s. In 1994 the first multiracial elections were held, and Nelson Mandela (b. 1918) became president of the newly democratic South Africa under black majority rule. Considering the divisions of the apartheid era, the social structure of the new South Africa is fairly harmonious, although crime is a problem.

Economy

It was South Africa's gold and diamond resources that originally attracted so many European settlers, and these commodities still account for about half the country's exports. Manufacturing is a growing sector of the economy, providing about one-quarter of export earnings. By contrast, agriculture accounts for only a small percentage of GDP. Maize/corn is the chief staple, while export crops include fruit, cotton, and tobacco. Livestock is also exported. Compared with other African countries, South Africa is modern, stable, and dynamic with a good infrastructure; the country has the best and most modern telephone system in Africa, for example. It also has well-developed legal and financial systems. Although there is a black government, many whites have remained or returned to the country, and the skills that helped forge a successful economy have remained in place. However, South Africa has high unemployment, HIV/AIDS is rife (over 20 percent of the population suffers from it) and daunting economic problems remain from the apartheid era, especially poverty among the disadvantaged groups.

many big game species—is under threat, and most is found in reserves such as the Kruger National Park.

Society

The first white settlers were Dutch Afrikaners, or Boers (farmers). As they moved inland they clashed with indigenous people such as the Bantu. In 1814 the British purchased the Cape Colony and began to conquer Bantu territories. They also fought two wars with the Boers before defeating them. In 1920 South Africa became a dominion. In 1948 the Afrikaner-backed National Party came to power and began the policy of apartheid. In the face of continuing opposition to apartheid, the government had softened its stance

THE SOUTH AFRICAN PEOPLE

Almost three-quarters of the population are blacks, generally of Bantu ancestry, the largest groups being the Zulu, the Xhosa, and the Sotho. The whites make up less than one-fifth of the overall population; they are mostly the descendants of European settlers, and the majority of them are Afrikaners—Dutch who arrived in the 17th century. The coloreds are people of mixed-race origins, and they form about one-tenth of the population. There is also a small Asian minority, mostly of Indian descent. This collection of different races has recently given rise to the term the "Rainbow Nation."

SWAZILAND

Swaziland borders Mozambique to the northeast but is otherwise enclosed by South Africa. The landscape descends in a series of steps from the mountainous High Veld to the Lebombo Escarpment in the east. Numerous rivers have cut deep gorges. The climate is subtropical but becomes wetter and cooler with increasing altitude. Grasslands and plantations of pine and eucalyptus flourish on the High Veld. On lower land woodland savanna is the typical vegetation. Wildlife includes leopards, hippos, antelopes, and giraffes.

The Swazis of southern Africa were guaranteed autonomy by the British in the late 19th century, and independence was achieved in 1968. Popular unrest has been caused by the monarchy's reluctance to introduce political reform and greater democracy. Swaziland has the world's highest known rates of HIV/AIDS infection—nearly 39 percent of the adult population is infected.

Subsistence agriculture employs most of the population. Cash crops such as sugarcane, citrus fruits, and tobacco are produced by European-controlled companies and by Swazis on resettlement schemes. Mining has declined in importance in recent years, with only coal and quarry-stone mines remaining active, but the manufacturing sector has diversified since the mid-1980s. Swaziland depends heavily on South Africa, from which it receives about nine-tenths of its imports and to which it sends nearly three-quarters of its exports. Wages sent back from workers employed in South Africa help boost income. The government is trying to encourage foreign investment. Recent droughts resulted in more than one-quarter of the population needing emergency food aid.

Swazi women wearing typical Swazi color prints. The Swazi make up over 80 percent of the country's population.

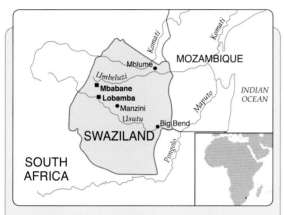

NATIONAL DATA – SWAZILAND

Land area	17,203 sq km (6,642 sq mi)			

Climate	Altitude m (ft)	Temperatures January °C(°F)	July °C(°F)	Annual precipitation mm (in)
Mbabane	1,145 (3,757)	20 (68)	12 (54)	1,442 (56.7)

Major physical features highest point: Emlembe 1,862 m (6,109 ft)

Population (2006 est.) 1,136,334

Form of government monarchy with two legislative houses

Armed forces no armed forces

Largest cities Mbabane (administrative – 81,312); Lobamba (legislative – 4,819)

Official languages Swazi, English

Ethnic composition Swazi 84.3%; Zulu 9.9%; Tsonga 2.5%; Indian 1.6%; others 1.7%

Religious affiliations Zionist 40% (a combination of Christianity and traditional ancestor worship), Roman Catholic 20%; Muslim 10%; Anglican, Bahai, Methodist, Mormon, Jewish and other 30%

Currency 1 lilangeni (SZL) = 100 cents

Gross domestic product (2006 est.) U.S. $5.91 billion

Gross domestic product per capita (2006 est.) U.S. $5,200

Life expectancy at birth male 32.1 yr; female 33.17 yr

Major resources asbestos, coal, clay, cassiterite, hydropower, forests, small gold and diamond deposits, quarry stone, citrus fruits, maize/corn, sugarcane, timber, tobacco

LESOTHO

Lesotho's vegetation includes alpine species on the higher ground, grassland on mountain slopes, and woodland in remote valleys.

NATIONAL DATA – LESOTHO

Land area	30,355 sq km (11,720 sq mi)			

Climate		Temperatures		Annual
	Altitude m (ft)	January °C(°F)	July °C(°F)	precipitation mm (in)
Maseru	1,528 (5,013)	21 (70)	8 (46)	725 (28.5)

Major physical features highest point: Thabana Ntlenyana 3,482 m (11,425 ft)

Population (2006 est.) 2,022,331

Form of government constitutional monarchy

Armed forces army 2,000

Capital city Maseru (115,559)

Official languages Sesotho, English

Ethnic composition Sotho 99.7%; Europeans, Asians, and other 0.3%

Religious affiliations Christian 80%; traditional beliefs 20%

Currency 1 loti (LSL) = 100 lisente; 1 South African rand (ZAR) = 100 cents

Gross domestic product (2006 est.) U.S. $5.195 billion

Gross domestic product per capita (2006 est.) U.S. $2,600

Life expectancy at birth male 35.55 yr; female 33.21 yr

Major resources water, diamonds, sand, clay, building stone, clothing, asparagus, beans, livestock, maize/corn, pulses, wheat, mohair, wool, leather, jute

Lesotho is surrounded by South Africa. More than 80 percent of the land is 1,800 m (5,905 ft) above sea level. Lesotho's highest point, Thabana Ntlenyana, is the highest point in southern Africa. South Africa's longest river, the Orange (Gariep) River, rises in the mountains of central-northern Lesotho. To the west the land forms a more fertile plateau. The climate is warm-temperate, but winters in the highlands are bitterly cold.

Basutoland was renamed the Kingdom of Lesotho on independence from Britain in 1966. After 23 years of military rule a constitutional government was restored in 1993, and exiled King Moshoeshoe II (1938–96) was reinstated in 1995. Violence erupted in 1998 following a disputed election, but constitutional reforms have since restored political stability. Lesotho's income comes mainly from wages sent back by nationals working in South African mines and from customs duties. A major hydroelectric power scheme enables the country to sell water to South Africa. A small manufacturing industry exploits local products, including canning, milling, leather, and jute industries. Clothing assembly is a growing sector. Subsistence agriculture has limited value in Lesotho, even though many people engage in it.

MAYOTTE

Mayotte, the most southeasterly island of the Comoros archipelago, is a French dependency; the other islands in the group form an independent republic. Covering an area of 374 sq km (144 sq mi), the land is generally mountainous with volcanic peaks and deep ravines, and the coast is fringed with coral reefs. The capital, Dzaoudzi, is perched on a rocky outcrop. The island is densely populated, with the majority of the people being Malagasy in origin. They speak Comorian, which is closely related to Swahili. Islam is the main religion (introduced to the island by Arab traders), although there is a Roman Catholic minority.

Along with all the other islands in the Comoros group, Mayotte was ceded to France in 1843, but when Comoros declared independence from France in 1975 Mayotte voted to remain French. Comoros still claims the island, supported by a 1979 UN resolution, but in 1984 France abandoned plans to return Mayotte to Comoros because of local opposition. The island has its own elected assembly but is also represented in the French parliament. The island is valued by France as a naval base. The economy, which relies heavily on France for food imports and financial aid, is mainly agricultural, with the main cash crops being vanilla, ylang-ylang (used in perfume), coconuts, and coffee. Manufacturing is largely restricted to food processing. The education system includes both Islamic and French schools.

RÉUNION

Réunion, the most southerly of the Mascarene islands, lies in the Indian Ocean, east of Madagascar and southwest of Mauritius. Réunion covers an area of 2,512 sq km (970 sq mi) and has a rugged and mountainous landscape with coastal plains. Like its close neighbor, Mauritius, Réunion has an active volcano—Piton de la Fournaise, the island's highest point. The rich rain forest that once covered the island has all but gone—along with much of the wildlife— although pockets remain in uninhabitable upland areas.

Réunion has been an overseas department of France since 1946, although it was first settled by French colonists who brought African slaves with them to work their sugar plantations. They were followed by influxes

of Malagasy, Chinese, and Indian laborers. The present population is mainly Creole, or mixed race. The economy is based on agriculture, especially sugarcane, which may account for over 80 percent of exports. Other cash crops include tobacco, vanilla, fruit, and vegetables. Manufacturing is mainly confined to food processing. Tourism is an increasing source of income.

SAINT HELENA

The remote volcanic island of St. Helena lies about 1,930 km (47 sq mi) off the southwest coast of Africa. It is a British colony which itself has two dependencies—

the strategically important Ascension Island to the northwest and the island group of Tristan da Cuhna to the southeast. St. Helena is about 120 sq km (47 sq mi) in area and is rugged and volcanic, with scattered plateaus and plains. Enough fertile land exists to support a small farming economy for its 7,000 or so inhabitants. The island is where French emperor Napoleon Bonaparte was exiled by the British from 1815 until his death in 1821. The main port and capital, Jamestown, is also the administrative center for Ascension Island and Tristan da Cuhna. St. Helena and several other islands are important wildlife havens.

An ancient cannon battery overlooking the sea at Réunion. Réunion was first colonized by the French in 1638, although between 1810 and 1815 it belonged to Britain.

Barren, rocky Ascension Island is a vital link across the South Atlantic. Many of its inhabitants are service personnel or communications workers. The Tristan da Cuhna group of islands includes, apart from Tristan da Cuhna itself, Inaccessible Island, Gough Island, and the three Nightingale Islands. Tristan da Cuhna is a volcanic cone that last erupted in 1961 and was settled again in 1963. It is the base for a small fishing industry.

GLOSSARY

Words in SMALL CAPITALS refer to other entries in the Glossary.

Amerindian A member of one of the many INDIGENOUS PEOPLES of Central and South America.

Anglican A member of the PROTESTANT church—founded in England in the 16th century—including the Church of England and other churches throughout the world.

apartheid A way of organizing society to keep racial groups apart. Introduced after 1948 in South Africa by the National Party to ensure continued white political dominance, it has now been dismantled.

Buddhism A religion founded in India in the 6th and 5th centuries B.C. and based on the teachings of Gautama Siddhartha (c. 563-483 B.C.), the Buddha, or "Awakened One."

cereal A cultivated grass selectively bred to produce high yields of edible grain for consumption by humans and livestock. The most important are wheat (*Triticum*), rice (*Oryza sativa*), and maize/corn (*Zea mays*).

Christianity A religion based on the teachings of Jesus Christ and originating from JUDAISM in the 1st century A.D. Its main beliefs are found in the Bible, and it is now the world's most widespread religion, divided into a number of churches and sects, including ROMAN CATHOLICISM, PROTESTANTISM, and ORTHODOX CHURCHES.

Communism A social and economic system based on the communal ownership of property. It usually refers to the STATE-controlled social and economic systems in the former Soviet Union and Soviet bloc countries and in the People's Republic of China.

Confucianism A religion or moral code based on the teachings of the Chinese philosopher Confucius (c. 551-479 B.C.) that formed the foundations of Chinese imperial administration and ethical behavior; also followed in Korea and other east Asian countries.

constitution The fundamental statement of laws that defines the way a country is governed.

constitutional monarchy A form of government with a hereditary head of STATE or monarch and a CONSTITUTION.

democracy A form of government in which policy is made by the people (direct democracy) or on their behalf (indirect democracy). Indirect democracy usually takes the form of competition among political parties at elections.

Dependency (1) A territorial unit under the jurisdiction of another STATE but not formally annexed to it. **(2)** An unequal economic or political relationship between two states or groups of states, in which one side is dependent on and supports the other.

ethnic group A group of people sharing a social or cultural identity based on language, religion, customs and/or common descent or kinship.

EU (European Union) An alliance of European NATIONS formed to agree common policies in the areas of trade, aid, agriculture, and economics.

exports Goods or services sold to other countries.

federalism A form of CONSTITUTIONAL government in which power is shared between two levels—a central, or federal, government and a tier of provincial or STATE governments.

GDP (Gross Domestic Product) The total value of a country's annual output of goods and services with allowances made for depreciation.

Hinduism A religion originating in India in the 2nd millennium B.C. It emphasizes mystical contemplation and ascetic practices that are closely interwoven with much of Indian culture.

indigenous peoples The original inhabitants of a region.

Islam A religion based on the revelations of God to the prophet Muhammad in the 7th century A.D., as recorded in the Qu'ran. It teaches submission to the will of God and is practiced throughout the Middle East, North Africa, and parts of Southeast Asia.

Judaism A religion that developed in ancient Israel based on God's law and revelations declared to Moses on Mount Sinai.

Methodism A PROTESTANT denomination of the CHRISTIAN church based on the teachings of the English theologian John Wesley (1703-91).

monarch A form of rule where there is a hereditary head of STATE.

Muslim An adherent of ISLAM.

nation A community that believes it consists of a single people, based on historical and cultural criteria.

nation-state A STATE in which the inhabitants all belong to one NATION. Most states claim to be nation-states; in practice almost all of them include minority groups.

Native American The INDIGENOUS PEOPLES of North America.

official language The language used by governments, schools, courts, and other official institutions in countries where the population has no single common mother tongue.

one-party state A political system in which there is no competition to the government party at elections, as in COMMUNIST and military regimes.

parliamentary democracy A political system in which the legislature (Parliament) is elected by all the adult members of the population and the government is formed by the party that commands a majority in the Parliament.

Protestant Term describing CHRISTIAN denominations that share a common rejection of the authority of the pope as head of the church, and of many ROMAN CATHOLIC practices.

Roman Catholic The largest of the CHRISTIAN churches, headed by the pope in Rome. It traces its origin and authority to St. Peter, one of the disciples of Jesus Christ and the first bishop of Rome. There are believers on all continents.

Shi'ite Muslim A member of the smaller of the two main divisions of ISLAM. Followers recognize Muhammad's son-in-law, Ali, and his descendants, the imams (prayer leaders), as his true successors and legitimate leaders of Islam.

state The primary political unit of the modern world, usually defined by its possession of sovereignty over a territory and its people.

subtropical The climatic zone between the TROPICS and TEMPERATE zones. There are marked seasonal changes of temperature but it is never very cold.

Sunni Muslim A member of the larger of the two main divisions of ISLAM. Its members recognize the Caliphs as the successors to Muhammad and follow the *sunna*, or way of the prophet, as recorded in the *hadithw*, the teachings of Muhammad.

temperate climate Any one of the climatic zones in mid-latitudes, with a mild climate. They cover areas between the warm TROPICS and cold polar regions.

tropics (tropical) The area between the Tropic of Cancer (23°30'N) and the Tropic of Capricorn (23°30'S), marking the lines of latitude farthest from the equator where the Sun is still found directly overhead at midday in midsummer.

FURTHER REFERENCES

General Reference Books

Allen, J. L., *Student Atlas of World Geography*, McGraw-Hill, Columbus, OH, 2004.

Atlas of World Geography, Rand McNally, Chicago, IL, 2005.

Baines, J. D., Egan, V., and G. Bateman, *The Encyclopedia of World Geography: A Country by Country Guide*, Thunder Bay, San Diego, CA, 2003.

de Blij, H. J., and P. O. Muller, *Concepts and Regions in Geography*, John Wiley & Sons, New York, 2004.

Muller, P. O., and E. Muller-Hames, *Geography, Study Guide: Realms, Regions, and Concepts*, John Wiley & Sons, New York, 2005.

Oxford Atlas of the World, Oxford University Press, New York, 2003.

Parsons, J. (ed.), *Geography of the World*, DK Children, London and New York, 2006.

Peoples of the World: Their Cultures, Traditions, and Ways of Life, National Geographic, Washington, DC, 2001.

Pulsipher, L. M., *World Regional Geography: Global Patterns, Local Lives*, W. H. Freeman, New York, 2005.

Warf, B. (ed.), *Encyclopedia of Human Geography*, Sage Publications, London and New York, 2006.

Specific to this volume

Adams, W. A., Goudie, A., and A. Orme (eds.), *The Physical Geography of Africa*, Oxford University Press, New York, 1999.

Glasse, C., and H. Smith (eds.), *New Encyclopedia of Islam*, AltaMira Press, Walnut Creek, CA, 2003.

Hetfield, J., *The Maasai of East Africa*, Rosen Publishing Group, New York, 2003.

Middleton, J. (ed.), *Africa: An Encyclopedia for Students*, Charles Scribner's Sons, New York, 2001.

Morris, P., Barrett, A., Murray, A., and M. Smits van Oyen, *Wild Africa*, BBC, London, 2001.

Murray, J., *Africa: Cultural Atlas for Young People*, Facts On File, New York, 2007.

Shaw, I. (ed.), *The Oxford History of Ancient Egypt*, Oxford University Press, Oxford, UK, 2000.

Sheehan, S., *South Africa since Apartheid*, Hodder Wayland, London, 2002.

Struhsaker, T. T., *Ecology of an African Rain Forest*, University of Florida Press, Gainesville, FL, 1999.

The Diagram Group, *Encyclopedia of African Nations and Civilizations*, Facts On File, New York, 2003.

Thompson, L.., *A History of South Africa*, Yale University Press, New Haven, CT, 2001.

General Web Sites

www.ethnologue.com
A comprehensive guide to all the languages of the world.

www.factmonster.com/ipka/A0770414.html
Geography facts and figures for kids.

www.geographic.org
Information on geography for students, teachers, parents, and children.

www.odci.gov/cia/publications/factbook/index.html
Central Intelligence Agency factbook of country profiles.

ww.panda.org
World Wide Fund for Nature (WWF).

www.peoplegroups.org/default.aspx
Listing and information on major ethnic groups around the world.

www.worldatlas.com
A world atlas of facts, flags, and maps.

INDEX

Page numbers in **bold** refer to main entries; numbers in *italics* refer to illustrations.